CALLING THE KINGDOM REMNANT

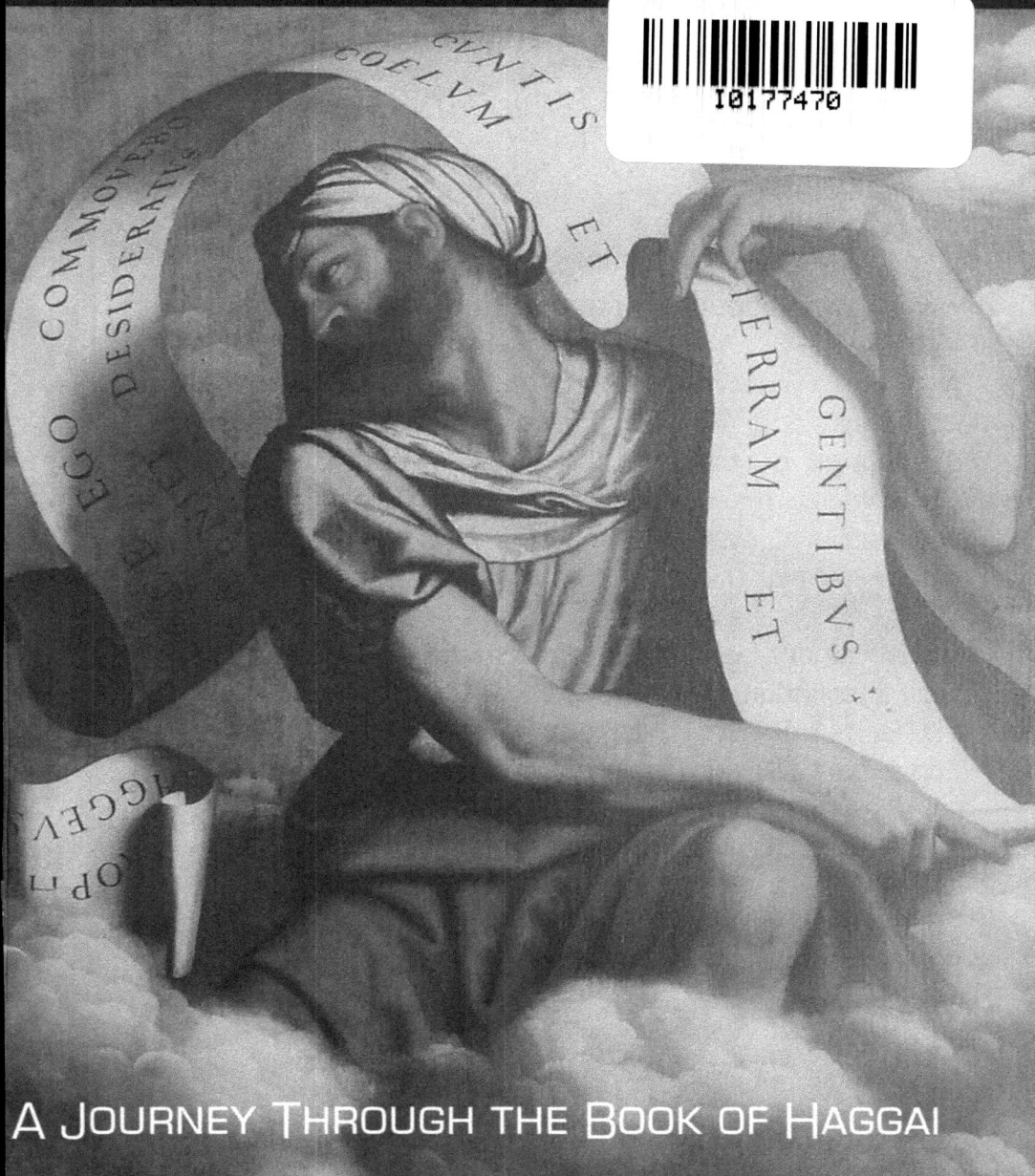

A JOURNEY THROUGH THE BOOK OF HAGGAI

Dr. Lee Ann B. Marino, Ph.D., D.Min., D.D.

CALLING THE KINGDOM REMNANT
A JOURNEY THROUGH THE BOOK OF HAGGAI

Dr. Lee Ann B. Marino, Ph.D., D.Min., D.D.

Published by:
Righteous Pen Publications
[An imprint of the Righteous Pen Publications Group]
www.righteouspenpublications.com

Book classification: Books > Religion & Spirituality > Christian Books & Bibles > Bible Study & Reference > Commentaries > Old Testament > Prophets

ISBN: 1940197244
13-Digit: 978-1940197-24-1

Printed in the United States of America.

Give us the heart of Abraham,
For changes make us bold;
And bless us only so that we
In turn may bless the world.

(*O God of the Eternal Now*,
Public Domain Hymn)

TABLE OF CONTENTS

ACKNOWLEDGEMENTS

I cannot publish this book on Haggai without acknowledging the powerful way in which the Lord inspired this particular writing on the book of Haggai. One day I was in prayer, and the Lord told me to write a commentary on the book of Haggai. At that point in time, I had written a total of one commentary, one on the book of Malachi. It never occurred to me to undertake a project to write about more than one book of the Bible at that time, and even though the publication of Malachi will follow this book, Malachi came first. What I imagined to be a short book became a powerful teaching tool with powerful impact on the revelations God wanted me to see in the book, to make the work of ministry greater.

So, in acknowledging for this book, I acknowledge my Lord, Jesus Christ. I thank Him for moving in my life and for, as difficult as it sometimes is, for seeing me through the ins and outs of this ministry, and for giving me my life, every day.

I also must thank the prayer warriors and intercessors who are under this ministry, praying for it, helping it to function, and helping it to work, day in and day out, in one form or another. I know it is the prayers of the faithful in this ministry that help us to see ourselves through to another day and another victory in Him.

Last, but certainly not least, I thank all those who are in helps in one form or another, because I know from experience how difficult of a job helps ministry can be. You are greatly loved and appreciated and we know that no matter how great a king in a kingdom, no matter how great a government may be in might or power, great things are always accomplished with the assistance of those who dedicate themselves to help.

FOREWORD

I first heard mention of the book of Haggai many years ago during a sermon preached by a woman at a very small church in Upstate New York. Even now, I remember the word she preached. I remember she talked a lot about finances and giving money to the church, and about God providing for her as she gave to Him. At the time, the message didn't resonate with me. I agreed that we should provide for God's work, but I felt she missed something in the translation of Haggai. I wasn't sure what was missing at the time, but even then, I believed Haggai was about more than a financial arrangement. I felt her message was a ploy to get people to put more money in the collection plate. Though she wasn't a bad speaker, she didn't seem to have much effect on those who heard her message.

The woman who preached this message on Haggai never became well-known. I am not sure where she is today. Even though her message did not resonate with me, I still give her great credit for daring to take on the challenge present in the book of Haggai. To this very day, I have never heard another message about the book of Haggai and given the situations we see in today's church, I am not bewildered as to why its contents remain largely unpopular.

The book of Haggai is one of the shortest books in the Bible. It is seldom studied, almost never examined for preaching, and often overlooked in the face of other prophetic books. Some modern theologians and preachers regard its contents as merely historical, with no modern relevance. Such an attitude diminishes the book's content, making it irrelevant for us. As Haggai is a part of God's Word, its contents are certainly far from irrelevant.

In my book, *Turning the Hearts of the Leaders Toward the Father: A Journey Through the Book of Malachi*, I raise the issue that we, as Christians, have our favorite passages and favorite books. Haggai is seldom listed as someone's favorite Bible book. Its contents are truly edifying, because the book of Haggai teaches and encourages us to make the Kingdom of God a priority. At the same time, its contents are severely convicting. Haggai exposes a common reality many wish to ignore. Merely claiming to set first the Kingdom of God as a priority is not enough.

Modern churches are full of people who have made a half-commitment to God and His Kingdom. It is their hope that they can just give enough to God so they can get what they desire out of life. They do not truly seek the Kingdom of God and His righteousness, but only the hand of God for things. In the process, they are totally missing the essentials of commitment and duty that lead to a deep and fulfilling life in our Lord.

God is calling every believer to examine their Kingdom walk and come to a place where what we desire in God is deeper than just having our needs met. God seeks every believer to grow in their commitment with Him to the point of relationship beyond debt and debtor. It is here that the book of Haggai takes on a powerful new meaning in light of our modern church. In Haggai's day, the Israelites have returned from exile. Their priority, however, is not getting God's house in order; it is rebuilding and expanding their own lives. In their fervor to have the best for themselves, God's ministry falls into ruin.

Haggai reveals the selfish nature of the Israelites in his day, and the selfishness of today's church. Too often Christians believe ministry work is about leaders and, therefore, make no commitment to the work of God. Haggai does not just give responsibility to the leaders to take responsibility for God's ministry but gives everyone who benefits from the Kingdom of God to step up and be responsible for it. People who call themselves Christians cannot be spectators, takers, receivers, and not give something back. Haggai's call to step back, review one's own conduct, and stand in God's call to make His

Kingdom a priority is both powerful and challenging to today's Christian community.

This study of Haggai is a text for all Christians. Anyone who claims to be a member of God's Kingdom must assess their Kingdom participation and service with God's requirements. If we are not measuring up in some way, we must meet God's challenge to action. In this short, simple message, we learn powerful precepts about God's financial expectations of believers, the priority of ministry needs in the life of every Kingdom member, the reality of Christian representation, and the reality of personal ruin when one does not participate actively in the Kingdom of God.

As a leader in the Kingdom, I encourage all believers engaging in this study to be honest with themselves. We need to take an inventory of ourselves and our lives. Where are we in our relationship with God? We have sought many things: do we have them? Are we happy with what we receive? Are we at peace with where we are with God, or do we seek more of Him? Is having many things what will bring Kingdom purpose? Are we walking in our Kingdom purpose? How can we bring the Kingdom of God into a greater focus and priority? In asking and honestly answering these questions, we can read Haggai's prophetic words with illumination and develop a deeper understanding of our call as Kingdom people.

e mei labium electum ut inuocent oms i noie
... iuraht ei bruo uno ult flumina tū ti
rel mei filij displor meor deferent munꝰ m̄
illa ꝶ cōfundif ei cunctis admuentolbꝫ tuis ꝗ
iuraitā el m̄ me quia ꝶ auferam de medio
magniloquos tebie tue ⁊ ꝶ adiciet exaltari ā
el m̄ monte seō meo ⁊ delinqua m̄ medio tui po
um paupem ⁊ egenum ⁊ spabut m̄ noie dm̄ re
ue ult̃ nō facient iniquitatem nec loquentur
acium ⁊ ꝶ muenietur m̄ ore eor linguadolo
ꝶ ipi pascentur ⁊ accubabunt ⁊ ꝶ erit q̄ ex
ꝶ hꝰ dicit dominus lauda filia syon iubila filia
m̄ letare ⁊ exulta ult̃ m̄ omni corde filia iertm̄
tulit dm̄ iudicium tuum auertit inimicos tuos
ult̃ dm̄ m̄ medio tui ꝶ timeb̃ malum ult̃ m̄
illa dicet iertm̄ noli timere syon nō dissoluatur
manus tua dm̄ deus tuus m̄ medio tui fortis ipe sal
uit gaudebit sup te m̄ letitia silebit m̄ dilectōe ⁊
exultabit sup te m̄ laude nugas qui alegꝫ recesse
⁊ congregabo qꝫ ex te erant ⁊ nō habes ultra sup eis
obprium ecce ego interficiam oms ꝗ aflixerunt te m̄
dicunt te m̄ tempore illo ⁊ saluabo claudicant
m̄ eam ꝗ eiecta fuerat congregabo ⁊ ponam eos m̄
laudem ⁊ m̄ nomen ⁊ omni terra confusiōis eor
m̄ illo tempore quo adducam uos ⁊ m̄ tempore quo congregabo
⁊ dabo uos m̄ nomen ⁊ m̄ laudem oibꝫ

tpl restauratōi ieiurm̄ aduentu
credulitatem ipli uellent intra
p eum ipli hnt diem ꝶ dum re
domus dei omnia ā ꝗ uertit h
reuileōem ipli edificatōem templ
at obseruantiam sacerdotalem
eor significant incipit liber

si anno secdo darij regis p san
at sem e librum domini m̄ mar
zpbabel filium salathiel ducer
iosedech sacerdotem magnum
eiicens ipli iste dic n̄
dm̄ edificandes sem e librum
zpbe dicens sic xpꝰ uob e ⁊
 gatis ⁊ domui ista destrah ⁊ ui
ꝓpte corda uestra ꝶ uias uestras
tulistis parum comedistis ⁊
til ꝶ estis inebriati operui
⁊ qui mercedes congregauit ⁊
ptulisti hꝰ dicit dominus ecce
uestras ꝶ uias uestras ascendite m̄
tia ⁊ edificate domum ⁊ accep
cabor dixit dominus respex
sem e munus ⁊ intulistis m̄ do
quam ob cam̄ dicit dm̄ exer
destra e ⁊ uos festinatis in de

INTRODUCTION

ABOUT THE BOOK OF HAGGAI

● ● ● ● ● ● ● ● ● ● ● ● ● ● ● ●

What are your responsibilities as a member of God's Kingdom? Even though it is unlikely you have ever heard a message from the book of Haggai, this little book is power-packed to reveal your responsibilities as a believer. For this reason, Haggai is very important and relevant for our day. It reveals to us our end of our covenant with God Almighty. For this reason, we must study Haggai to understand six key things:

- God's call to establish Kingdom priorities in the life of every believer.

- The nature of those Kingdom priorities as pertain to personal satisfaction and blessing, finances, participation in Kingdom ministry, obedience, work and labor, conduct, and holiness.

- There is great importance in paying careful attention to God's Word, that we may obey Him completely in everything; disobedience is equivalent to a defiled offering.

- God's glory abounds when His people prioritize for the Kingdom.

- There is a difference between seeking first the Kingdom of God and seeking the things we want, whatever they may be, through God's Kingdom.

- God has the power to uproot leaders and shake nations and establish those He has chosen in their place.

Position in the Bible

The book of Haggai is in a group of twelve prophetic writings classified as the "Minor Prophets." Its classification as such does not mean Haggai is in any way of minor consideration or worth, but that the contents of the prophecies are far shorter than those of Isaiah, Jeremiah, and Ezekiel. The book of Haggai follows the book of Zephaniah and precedes the book of Zechariah.

Length

The book of Haggai is two chapters long. Even in Bibles that sometimes number the verses differently, Haggai remains a two-chapter book, and the content is the same.

Author

The book of Haggai was written by the Prophet Haggai. His name means "my holiday."

About the author

Nothing is known about the life of the Prophet Haggai. Some believe he was one of the captives of the Babylonian Captivity. He began his ministry sixteen years after the Jewish return to Judah, around 520 B.C. He was the first of three Old Testament prophets (the other two being Zechariah and Malachi) who were a part of this period in history.

Time written

The book of Haggai was written around 520 B.C. It was approximately eighteen years after Persia conquered Babylon under the rule of Cyrus (538 B.C.) and the Jewish captives were permitted to return to Judah.

Who is Haggai for?

Haggai's prophecy applies to all believers. In his day, the Prophet Haggai addressed the nation of Israel as it had returned from exile. Today we understand the book to apply to Christian believers, now redeemed through Christ to live in God's Kingdom. It is a book of thorough principle and discipline. Haggai is a word of correction for Kingdom believers who errantly assume God's promises come without obligation or commitment on their part. It addresses Christians on all practical levels to regard and edify God's Kingdom with their commitment and resources.

The book of Haggai is also a rallying cry to action and interest in Christian ministry. While it is true God's leaders are called to Christian ministry, it is also true that all God's people are called to participate in Christian ministry. Haggai reminds us that God's purpose and interest in His people is beyond the meeting of needs into the realm of Kingdom activity and dominion. If we want to participate in this, we must step up and act in accord with God's covenant principles.

History

The book of Haggai was after Jewish captives were permitted to return to Judah, somewhere around 520 BC. This prophecy comes approximately eighteen years after the declaration was made permitting their return, which indicates the Jews residing in Judah had several years to straighten their circumstances and focus on rebuilding God's ministry. We can see from Haggai and other prophetic writings from this similar time frame (Zechariah, Ezra, Nehemiah, and Malachi) that God's people returned lazy, preoccupied with worldly things, and seeking after themselves.

Haggai's cry to rebuild the temple and, therefore, reestablish God's ministry, was one of God's first shifts toward reestablishing a Kingdom mindset within His people during a transitional time.

Context

Haggai's prophecy is a call to first things: for the people of God to seek first His Kingdom and His righteousness and then watch their lives fall into place. This book speaks to the character of Kingdom people. It clarifies that suffering or difficult circumstances are no excuse to refrain from Kingdom priorities. Haggai calls for the people of God to attend to first things, and keeping God and His Kingdom as the first priority of their lives.

In a unique way, Haggai addresses the issue of covenant as part of God's Kingdom. Covenant is not just about God's doings. Many today teach God to be faithful to His covenant no matter what we do or do not do. Covenant is not, in actuality, that simple. We either accept God's covenant and abide by its precepts, or we do not. If we do not abide by covenant, we have broken the covenant and are no longer heirs to its promises. Haggai focuses in deeply on obedience through priority setting, and causes us to recognize the depth of covenant promise on our end. In developing a deeper understanding of obedience, all believers come to a greater understanding of what's expected of them as members of God's Kingdom.

CHAPTER ONE

THE KINGDOM OF GOD IS YOUR FIRST PRIORITY (HAGGAI CHAPTER 1)

Key verses

- **Verses 5-6**: *Now this is what the LORD Almighty says: "Give careful thought to your ways. You have planted much, but have harvested little. You eat, but never have enough. You drink, but never have your fill. You put on clothes, but are not warm. You earn wages, only to put them in a purse with holes in it."*

- **Verses 10-11**: *"Therefore, because of you the heavens have withheld their dew and the earth its crops. I called for a drought on the fields and the mountains, on the grain, the new wine, the oil and whatever the ground produces, on men and cattle, and on the labor of your hands."*

- **Verse 13**: Then *Haggai, the LORD's messenger, gave this message of the LORD to the people: "I am with you," declares the LORD*

Words and phrases to know

- **Word of the Lord**: From two Hebrew words: *dabar* which means "speech, word, thinking, thing;"[1] and *Yehovah* which means "the existing One; the proper Name of the one true God."[2]

- **Prophet Haggai**: From two Hebrew words: *nabiy'* which means "spokesman, speaker, prophet;"[3] and *Chaggay* which means "festive; 10th in order of the Minor Prophets; first prophet to prophecy after the captivity."[4]

- **Zerubbabel**: From the Hebrew word *Zerubbabel* which means "sown in Babylon; the grandson of King Jehoiachin and leader of the first group of returning exiles from Babylon."[5]

- **Joshua**: From the Hebrew word *Yehowshuwa'* which means "Jehovah is salvation; son of Jehozodak and high priest after the restoration."[6]

- **Time**: From the Hebrew word *'eth* which means "time."[7]

- **House**: From the Hebrew word *bayith* which means "house; place; receptacle; home; house as containing a family; household, family; household affairs; inwards (metaphorically); temple; on the inside prep; within."[8]

- **Built**: From the Hebrew word: *banah* which means "to build, rebuild, establish, cause to continue."[9]

- **Paneled**: From the Hebrew word *caphan* which means "to cover, cover in, wainscotted, covered with boards or paneling."[10]

- **Ruin**: From the Hebrew word *chareb* which means "waste, desolate, dry."[11]

- **Give careful thought to your ways**: From two Hebrew words: *suwm* which means "to put, place, set, appoint, make;"[12] and *derek* which means "way, road, distance, journey, manner."[13]

- **Planted**: From the Hebrew word *zara'* which means "to sow, scatter seed."[14]

- **Harvested little**: From two Hebrew words: *bow* which means, "to go in, enter, come, go, come in;"F[15] and *'me'at* which means "littleness, few, a little, fewness."[16]

- **Eat**: From the Hebrew word *'akal* which means "to eat, devour, burn up, feed."[17]

- **Never have enough**: From the Hebrew word *sob'ah* which means "satisfaction, satiety, one's fill."[18]

- **Drink**: From the Hebrew word *shathah* which means "to drink."[19]

- **Never have your fill**: From the Hebrew word *shakar* which means "to be or become drunken, be intoxicated."[20]

- **Put on clothes**: From the Hebrew word *labash* which means "to dress, wear, clothe, put on clothing, be clothed."[21]

- **Not warm**: From the Hebrew word *chom* which means "heat, hot."[22]

- **Wages**: From the Hebrew word *sakar* which means "to hire."[23]

- **Purse with holes in it**: From two Hebrew words: *tserowr* which means "bundle, parcel, pouch, bag (as in packed);"[24] and *naqab* which means "to pierce, perforate, bore, appoint; to curse, blaspheme."[25]

- **Pleasure**: From the Hebrew word: *ratsah* which means "to be pleased with, be favorable to, accept favorably."[26]

- **Be honored**: From the Hebrew word *kabad* which means "to be heavy, be weighty, be grievous, be hard, be rich, be honorable, be glorious, be burdensome, be honored."[27]

- **Much**: From the Hebrew word *rabah* which means "be or become great, be or become many, be or become much, be or become numerous; to shoot."[28]

- **Little**: From the Hebrew word *me'at* which means "littleness, few, a little, fewness."[29]

- **Brought home**: From two Hebrew words: *bow'* which means "to go in, enter, come, go, come in;"[30] and *bayith* which means "house; place; receptacle; home, house as containing a family; household, family; household affairs; inwards (metaphor); temple (adverb); on the inside (preposition); within."[31]

- **Blew away**: From the Hebrew word *naphach* which means "to breathe, blow, sniff at, seethe, give up or lose (life)."[32]

- **Busy**: From the Hebrew word *ruwts* which means "to run."[33]

- **Heavens**: From the Hebrew word *shamayim* which means "heaven, heavens, sky."[34]

- **Earth**: From the Hebrew word *'erets* which means "land, earth."[35]

- **Drought**: From the Hebrew word *choreb* which means "dryness, desolation, drought, heat."[36]

- **Fields and mountains**: From two Hebrew words: *'eretz* which means "land, earth;"[37] and *har* which means "hill, mountains, hill country, mound."[38]

- **Grain**: From the Hebrew word *dagan* which means "wheat, cereal, grain, corn."[39]

- **New wine**: From the Hebrew word *tiyrowsh* which means "wine, fresh or new wine, must, freshly pressed wine."[40]

- **Oil**: From the Hebrew word *yitshar* which means "fresh oil, shining (pure) oil."[41]

- **Whatever the ground produces**: From two Hebrew words: *'adamah* which means "ground, land;"[42] and *yatsa'* which means "to go out, come out, exit, go forth."[43]

- **Men and cattle**: From two Hebrew words: *'adam* which means "man, mankind;"[44] and *behemah* which means "beast, cattle, animal."[45]

- **Labor of your hands**: From two Hebrew words: *yegiya'* which means "toil, work; product, produce, acquired property (as a result of work);"F[46] and *kaph* which means "palm, hand, sole, palm of the hand, hollow or flat of the land."[47]

- **Remnant**: From the Hebrew word *she'eriyth* which means "rest, residue, remainder, remnant."[48]

- **Obeyed**: From the Hebrew word *shama'* which means "to hear, listen to, obey; sound."[49]

- **Message**: From the Hebrew word *dabar* which means "speech, word, thinking, thing."[50]

- **Sent**: From the Hebrew word *shalach* which means "to send, send away, let go, stretch out."[51]

- **Feared**: From the Hebrew word *yare'* which means "to fear, revere, be afraid; to shoot, pour."[52]

13

- **Stirred up**: From the Hebrew word *'uwr* which means "to rouse one's self, awake, awaken, incite."[53]

Haggai 1:1-2

In the second year of King Darius, on the first day of the sixth month, the word of the LORD came through the prophet Haggai to Zerubbabel son of Shealtiel, governor of Judah, and to Joshua son of Jehozadak, the high priest.

This is what the LORD Almighty says: 'These people say, 'The time has not yet come for the LORD's house to be built.''

(Related Bible references: 1 Kings 17:7-16, 2 Kings 20:17-18, 1 Chronicles 3:17, 1 Chronicles 3:19-20, 1 Chronicles 6:15. Psalm 137:1,8, Ecclesiastes 3:1, Isaiah 13:19, Isaiah 21:9, Jeremiah 50:8, Jeremiah 51:6-7, Jeremiah 51:44-46, Ezekiel 18:30, Daniel 2:20-22, Hosea 10:12, Zechariah 2:7, Matthew 1:12-13, Matthew 3:2, Matthew 3:8, Matthew 7:16-20, Mark 1:15, Luke 3:27, John 15:2-4, Acts 2:38, Romans 13:1, 2 Corinthians 6:2, 16-18, Galatians 4:4-7, Galatians 5:22, Ephesians 4:7-13, Ephesians 5:15-16, Colossians 1:16, Revelation 14:6-13, Revelation 17:1-18, Revelation 18:1-24, Revelation 19:1-10)

One of the great themes of the book of Haggai is time. In a book of only two chapters, six different references are made to both the time frame of the first initial word and the progress of the prophetic action (Haggai 1:1, 1:15, 2:1, 2:10, 2:18, 2:20). Time is most relevant in the book of Haggai. The book's contents are all about the Kingdom of God and priorities. Connected to that is a wise use of time and resources, which was not a principle in place within the Israelites at the time. From the beginning, God has worked to mark time, contain time, and make time accessible, productive, and useful – and He expects no less from those who call themselves by His Name.

It's obvious from observing the book of Haggai that time is an important precept in the lives of believers. We are so busy talking about things such as money and how to get what we want in today's church, we have forgotten entirely about the precept of time, times and seasons, appointed times, and the urgency of meeting spiritual appointments. In understanding these terms, they mean the following:

- **Time:** Within a Biblical understanding, there's more than one concept of time. There is *chronos*, which relates to chronological time, or time as we might understand it. There is also *karios*, which we can understand as divine time, or eternity. While we understand time to happen in an order of events, spiritual time is understood to run in cycles. Those cycles connect us to prophecy; in that they relate to God's word to us throughout life. It also means that throughout life, we have the chance to make things right with God more than once (Ephesians 5:15-16).

- **Times:** Times refer to the general time frame of God's plan. The word for "times" is similar to *chronos*, but it's not as simple as describing such on a timetable. It's more about arranging certain events or happenings together for a divine purpose. I compare the idea of times to providence: somehow, in a way we don't understand, God's hand works behind all things in history. It doesn't always make sense to us, but God is still moving through a bigger plan than we can easily understand (Daniel 2:20-22).

- **Seasons:** If times are bigger, circumstantial orchestrations, then seasons are more interpersonal, interchangeable situations we all experience as part of our spiritual growth and development. Seasons work through people, places, and circumstances that change, much as natural seasons also change. These are cyclical in nature, as is spiritual time in a general sense (Ecclesiastes 3:1).

- **Appointed times:** An appointed time is one by which God appoints us to do or complete a specific assignment. Within an appointed time, God gives the ability and equipping to complete said assignment as part of a time or season (or sometimes both) (Galatians 4:4-7).

- **Spiritual appointments:** The concept that God establishes specific people along with specific circumstances to bring about His will. It is a place of divine intersection and overlapping (1 Kings 17:7-16).

In the instance of temple rebuilding, we can see divine time at work. Understanding times equated to recognizing a season, all of which coincided to create the appointed time for the temple's rebuilding. The timing of Israel's needed leadership along with Israel's needed self-examination spoke loudly that the time was then to do the Lord's will regarding ministry.

Israel, however, wasn't recognizing these signs on their own. Just as in Israel's day, believers today go through phases where time is not of the essence to them. Sometimes we are discouraged or despondent and believe we can delay the work of the Lord to another time. The more we delay, the more time goes by, and the more opportunities we miss.

We are living in the appointed time for ministry and discipleship. Living in the last days does not make us less responsible for ministry. If anything, it makes us more alert and more aware of God's Kingdom advancements. The time to attend to God's ministry is now, and it is wrong for us to delay God's work until another time. As Christians, one of our primary commands is to make disciples until the time when Jesus returns. The day (appointed time) for salvation is now, but that time will not last forever (2 Corinthians 6:2). God has appointed set and fixed times and seasons, and in this season, we can never be too attentive to the work of God's ministry. It is not an appointed season to delay, but to make sincere and serious haste.

Our first reference to time in Haggai sets the stage for us in history. We learn first from time reference that this book takes place after the Babylonian exile. The Israeli captives had returned to Judah after living in a long siege of captivity. It is obvious they were quite comfortable, having settled in and lived in Judah for several years prior to Haggai's prophecy.

The word *Haggai* means "festive."[54] As with all God's prophets, the name of Haggai reveals to us about his purpose and mission. Haggai came to the people of Israel, speaking God's word in a day and age where they declared themselves on sabbatical from God's work. Their personal rest and provision came before their God. Haggai declared the end to this season of absence from Kingdom principles, recognizing there is no festivity when one is absent from

God's Kingdom. His name also reminded God's people of the true importance in being festive for the Lord consistently, not needing a special holiday or occasion to do God's work. The time to start God's work is now, now is the day, and now is the hour, for the fullness of God's work to go forth. It is a joyous and festive thing to be about God's ministry, to have the unique privilege to proclaim and live the words, *Repent, for the Kingdom of heaven is near* (Ezekiel 18:30, Matthew 3:2, Mark 1:15, Acts 2:38).

Haggai's prophetic word came forth in an interesting way. It was not simply a random proclamation. As with all things divine, God had Haggai deliver the message through channels of order. The message was delivered to Zerubbabel, the governor of Judah, and Joshua, the high priest.

The name *Zerubbabel* literally means "sown in Babylon."[55] His name automatically indicates he was born in Babylon and therefore a citizen of the Babylonian nation. It is most interesting God specifically directed His message to one who was "sown in Babylon." The Bible often refers to Babylon in a negative light, a picture of fallen humanity, unrepentant sinfulness, and human evil (Psalm 137:1, 8, Isaiah 13:19, Isaiah 21:9, Jeremiah 50:8, Jeremiah 51:6-7). The nation of Israel itself went off to Babylon due to its own idolatries and returned in a great spiritual mess, worse than when they left. They sought divine redemption from captivity, but didn't pursue the things of God upon their return. Instead, their priorities were everything but the Kingdom of God. They made no priority or provision for God's ministry. Since Babylon is often the picture of sin beyond redemption, why did God choose to specifically send His message through a leader who was "sown in Babylon?"

History does not give much information about Zerubbabel. Almost everything we know about him comes from the Bible and Old Testament Apocryphal sources. The Bible tells us he was the son of Shealtiel, also a governor of Judah. He had several sons (Meshullam, Hananiah, Hashubah, Ohel, Berekiah, Hasadiah and Jushab-Hesed) and a daughter (Shelomith) (1 Chronicles 3:19-20). Zerubbabel is listed in the Gospels of Matthew and Luke as a descendant of Jesus (Matthew 1:12-13, Luke 3:27). In Sirach (a book of the Old Testament Deuterocanonicals), Zerubbabel is cited as part of the temple restoration, lauded as one who was "like a signet ring on the right hand" (Sirach 49:13). In the book of 1 Esdras, a book of the Old Testament Apocrypha, Zerubbabel is listed as one of the wisest men of Persia.[56]

The historical background we do have on Zerubbabel, however limited it is, proves he was a man of relevance. God used a man planted in a foreign land to be part of the lineage of Jesus Christ! By virtue of his name, many would assume God would never use Zerubbabel as a channel of authority. I venture God would use the man "sown in Babylon" for three reasons:

- **God establishes order (Romans 13:1, Colossians 1:16) and respects that order**: Sometimes we forget that God has placed divine order and authority in the world. Even though the people who fill God's appointed offices do not always act godly, that does not change the important role that office is to play in God's plan for order. We see in the New Testament that one of the first and primary concepts was God's establishment of order upon the ascension of Christ (Ephesians 4:7-13). God's established order does not always make sense to our concepts or worldly concepts. The people we may think are most likely to be used by God as authorities and preparers of His order may indeed not be the ones God chooses. What is most relevant, however, is God trusts those who trust Him. He establishes leaders who trust and obey Him and that He can use as vessels of His order.

- **There is redemption for those who "come out of Babylon" (Jeremiah 51:44-46, Revelation 18:4-8)**: Babylon is often used as an illustration of the world and the evils contained therein. It is also used as an illustration of false religious systems that pervert the truth and mislead God's people. For this reason, the Bible portrays God as calling His people out of Babylon (Jeremiah 51:44-46, Revelation 18:4-8). If we answer the call, repent, and turn to God, God redeems us, no matter what system we come from. Zerubbabel stood and continues to stand as a signpost of hope for all others who were "sown in Babylon" and those of us today who were similarly sown but have come out of Babylon into the Kingdom of God.

- **We cannot judge people based on their origins**: We can't assume God will call and use one person and not someone else because of where they come from or what they've come out from. Where people are "sown" has no relevance to where they are when they stand in Christ. Just because someone is born somewhere or under a certain spiritual system does not mean they have been sown under that system in their minds, beliefs, and hearts. The same is true in reverse: just because someone has grown up in church, lived and heard the truth, and was raised right does not mean the Spirit is sown in their minds, beliefs, and hearts. We must seek to see fruit, rather than history or ancestry (Hosea 10:12, Matthew 3:8, Matthew 7:16-20, John 15:2-4, Galatians 5:22).

For all these reasons, Zerubbabel was a perfect choice for leader of God's people and to receive the message of Haggai. He typifies solid leadership, redemption, and God's system of equality.

The other leader, Joshua, son of Jehozadak, was the high priest. Once again, we see a relevance in the names of the leaders: *Joshua* means "Jehovah is salvation."[57] The people of Israel needed to remember God was their salvation and follow a leader that embodied the necessary priestly intercession, character, and integrity to bring them back to the importance a Kingdom ministry mindset.

Haggai's prophecy opens in verse 2, quoting the LORD: *These people say, 'The time has not yet come for the LORD's house to be built.* God wastes no time in stating the issue at hand. The people of Israel decided it was not time to rebuild the temple, thus not re-establishing the work of the ministry in Judah. It was at their decision and decree, not God's decision. We see no evidence the people gave God's will any consideration in this decision; they just made the decision. In making such a decision, they chased after alternate priorities, placing other things before the Kingdom of God. They delayed the work of the ministry in the pursuit of themselves.

Haggai 1:3-6

Then the word of the LORD came through the prophet Haggai: "Is it a time for you yourselves to be living in your paneled houses, while this house remains a ruin?"

Now this is what the LORD Almighty says: "Give careful thought to your ways. You have planted much, but have harvested little. You eat, but never have enough. You drink, but never have your fill. You put on clothes, but are not warm. You earn wages, only to put them in a purse with holes in it."

[Related Bible references: Genesis 12:2, Psalm 33:12, Ezra 5:1, Hosea 10:12, Malachi 3:17, Matthew 4:4, Matthew 6:19-21, Matthew 6:33, Matthew 13:8, Matthew 13:19, Mark 4:14, Mark 4:15, Mark 4:20, John 4:10-14, John 4:37, John 6:25-59, John 10:10, Romans 13:14, 1 Corinthians 9:11, 2 Corinthians 4:7, Galatians 3:27, Galatians 6:7, Galatians 6:8, Ephesians 5:18, Colossians 3:12, 1 Timothy 6:19, James 3:18]

The people of Israel received stern correction from God through Haggai. It is obvious they were distracted. They were busy establishing houses, properties, and increasing themselves. They were working with their own gain in mind and were ignoring the Kingdom of God. As with all attitudes of this kind, they justified themselves by delaying God's work. As long as the ministry lay in ruin, it did not merit attention. A half-finished project merits finishing. A nearly finished project merits finishing. But to many...if it's never been started...out of sight, out of mind. If it hasn't been attended to yet...it can wait...until later.

The Israelites were guilty of a classic condition: they were seeking things through the Kingdom of God, rather than seeking first the Kingdom of God. Instead of being Kingdom people, truly understanding their Kingdom identity, the Israelites were seeking what they wanted through God. In the process of using God as a justification to seek things, they became idolaters (the ultimate god they served being themselves and selfishness). God's Word establishes we are to seek first the Kingdom of God and His righteousness, and all other things will come forth unto us (Matthew 6:33). They did not follow God's Kingdom order and instead sought all things in place of God's Kingdom. After all, they'd been exiled and had to do for themselves! They felt sorry for what had happened to them and wanted to compensate for the past. Things were the choice to fill the void. God's work could wait until they were established, comfortable, and had enough! They would get to the temple later.

"Comfortable" is the word that describes the mindset of these people. They were comfortable where they were. Is that not an appropriate word to describe believers today? Most people today seek things through the Kingdom. They want their husband or wife to be the spouse they've always dreamed of, a better job, a better car, a better house, more money, more trips, and more time off. They don't ascribe to be better believers or more serious in their walk with the Lord. As it stands today, most ministries are in financial ruin. Many ministers uphold jobs just to support the ministry work and vision while followers take from the vision without giving. The modern church lives in this mentality, never really becoming a part of God's Kingdom enough to belong but just having enough to see the vision of comfort and desire they seek.

Believers today live in a metaphorical exile. We live in Babylon and many errantly pursue Babylon, exiling themselves from God. Although they claim to want to come out of exile and live in God's Kingdom, what they really seek are Kingdom benefits. Kingdom living never makes the leap from desire to obedience. We need to do more than just desire the things God can give us and truly live as people who desire to know God and His righteousness. This is the difference between living with a view of God's Kingdom and truly living as a Kingdom citizen. When one visits a country, they have privileges to stay for a period of time, obeying the most basic rules to avoid having their trip cut short. They visit, experience some of the culture, eat some of the food, and then return home when their visa expires. Even though they've received a taste of the benefits that culture has to offer, they have no idea the conditions required to be a member of that nation. When one is a citizen of a country, they are required to live the culture, obey the rules, honor their cultural history, know the laws, and submit to the governance of that nation. The same is true when one is a true citizen of the Kingdom of God. We must live Kingdom culture, obey God's rules, honor our Kingdom history, know the laws and governance of God's Kingdom, and submit to God's leadership. Having a visa and taking a visit to the Kingdom of God every Sunday or every holiday does not give one the citizenship benefits of Kingdom living. While comfortable individuals may reap some of the benefits of Kingdom culture, living in true Kingdom citizenship establishes the ministry as primary and sets its citizens for life. Truly blessed is the nation (group of people set apart for Him, those He calls and chooses) whose God is the Lord! (Psalm 33:12) Comfortable visitors are not blessed, because they follow false gods. Even though Israel had things, they were not truly blessed and not fully receiving the benefits of the Kingdom.

Sixteen years had passed since the Israelites returned to Judah. They'd spent 16 years delaying God's work and putting themselves first, living as casual visitors to the Kingdom. This proves an attitude that delays God's work does not pass or improve with time. The more they sought after the wrong things, the more they sought things. There was never a convenient time to begin God's work again among the people. The Israelites weren't stupid. They knew when the temple work began, even more would be expected of them. They would have to attend to sacrifices, giving, festivals, and more diligently seek the Lord as His Kingdom people. Being comfortable and complacent wouldn't be enough anymore.

Being comfortable isn't enough for God's true people. We shouldn't seek to have enough of God to just get by and get what we want. We can see such laxity does not lead to the abundant life of Jesus Christ (John 10:10). As a seeking people, we should always desire to go beyond what is obvious and needed into what is truly purposeful and meaningful. Finding success in life means finding it as we walk in the ministry work God has appointed to us, while at the same time, supporting God's greater ministry present in His Kingdom.

Haggai's work reveals the true importance of prophecy and the office of the prophet. Prophets are people called to awaken, shaken, stir up, cause controversy, and speak God's Word so it convicts. If he had never come along, Israel would never have shaken itself out of its comforts and complacency. Such is still needed today in an increasingly comforted world. Prophets bring reality to a situation as they expose it for what it is. Whatever we seek is nothing if the Kingdom of God is not in front of it, in it, and behind it. Prophets are called to reveal God's will to His people, especially when they are not receiving that revelation.

This thought echoes in the words, "Give careful thought to your ways." The Israelites were deliberate in their actions. They knew what they wanted to do, but they hadn't given careful thought to the results of their ways. Even though they selfishly put themselves first, they weren't reaping the benefits of their actions. Despite this fact, they continued to seek themselves and delay the work of God's ministry. They kept at their ways even though they had no results.

There is great symbolism in Haggai's words to the people, beyond the obvious literal interpretation. To truly gain a profound understanding, we shall look at those deeper meanings:

- **Sown much but harvested little**: Sowing and reaping are basic Scriptural concepts (Hosea 10:12, Matthew 13:8, Mark 4:14, John 4:37, 1 Corinthians 9:11, Galatians 6:7, James 3:18). The Lord encourages us to sow and trust Him for harvest. It is possible, however, to sow and not reap, because we do not sow under the right circumstances (Matthew 13:19, Mark 4:15, Mark 4:20, Galatians 6:8). The people of Haggai's day put great effort into their crops. They sowed a lot of seed, spent their time working with the land to bring about a great harvest, but did not reap the benefits of that harvest. In a larger sense, the word "much" means "be or become great, be or become many, be or become much, be or become numerous; to shoot."[58] The people of Israel were sowing much - but they were sowing it in the wrong places. Instead of sowing into God, they were sowing into themselves. Rather than becoming great, as the Lord had prophesied over their ancestors (Genesis 12:2, Malachi 3:17), they were not expanding and growing as a people. Their stunted spiritual priorities led to a small harvest economically and a stunted growth of the people as a nation and as people themselves. As we sow, so shall we reap (Galatians 6:7).

- **Eat, but never have enough**: Years ago the Rolling Stones immortalized the words of gluttony: "I Can't Get No Satisfaction." Just like in the song, the Israelites tried, and they tried, and they tried, and they tried, and they tried...but they couldn't get what they wanted. The word "eat" means "to eat, devour, burn up, feed."[59] The word "never have enough" means "satisfaction, satiety, one's fill."[60] The people of Israel were bottomless pits. They ate, and ate, and ate, but were never filled because they lived in selfish gluttony. All they wanted was more. They were permanently empty because they did not have their necessary spiritual indwelling, the Holy Spirit living in them. Finding our necessary spiritual filling helps us to heal gluttony because we truly find what we need and seek in our lives. When we seek what we want through material things, we miss the true Bread of Life that satisfies, Jesus Christ (John 6:25-59). In a world seeking material things, it's easy to forget we do not sustain life on physical bread, but on God's Word as well (Matthew 4:4). In recognizing this, it's easy to see why the Israelites (and many today) lived with such intense hunger and were never satisfied.

- **Drink but never have your fill**: The English wording of this passage doesn't convey the essence of Haggai's words in the Hebrew. The Hebrew word for "never have your fill" means "to be or become drunken, be intoxicated."[61] In other words, the Israelites sought to get drunk but never accomplished their goal. God was giving the Israelites (and us today) an example of futility. They kept trying to do something, but never reached their goal, so it was pointless to keep doing it. Too many people today do the same, attempting to reach a certain state of being and are unable to reach it via their current means...yet they continue doing what they've always done. As God's people, we are not to be preoccupied with such futility. The Scriptures tell us not to be drunk on wine but to be filled with the Spirit (Ephesians 5:18). That which fills and satisfies us is not of this world and never leads us to futile things. Jesus is our ultimate living water, which satisfies any thirst we may have, and makes it so we do not thirst for drunkenness again (John 4:10-14). It is our privilege to join in the work of His ministry, as we have received the satisfaction we seek!

- **Put on clothes, but not warm**: It's amazing the way people can dress and disguise the truth about themselves. In ancient times, vanity was alive and well as it is today, and people were as interested in making the effective presentation rather than the right one. We have clothing to make you look thinner, fuller, more attractive, bring out skin tone or other features, and so on. We can look elegant, expensive, or practical. Clothing can be used to enhance who we are and draw more attention to the truth of God revealed in our lives. How we clothe ourselves can also be used to be deceptive. We can seek to give a false impression of where we are and where we're going, spending all our time worrying about external matters. We can wear clothes for impractical purposes and with motives other than practicality, hoping they will do the job, but find quickly we're cold when it's not warm out! Often, we find ourselves clothed in wrong things spiritually, bringing out impracticalities of faith and leaving ourselves vulnerable to spiritual cold. We are called to clothe ourselves in Jesus Christ (Romans 13:14, Galatians 3:27) and Christ's virtues of compassion, kindness, humility, gentleness and patience (Colossians 3:12). This way we ensure we will always be protected from outside elements.

- **Earn wages but put them in a purse with holes in it**: People throughout history have always thought the way to get money is to store it up and save it. In like thinking, the perceived sign of wealth is spending money on the things one wants to buy. The Israelites didn't have a problem with making money, they had a problem with keeping it. Those who worked for wages got their money…and then blew it. Sometimes it seems like the money we get today just goes right out the window, but often, closer inspection reveals questionable spending. It's not so much that money can't be found, but that priority is amiss. On the ministry front, we can sow into wrong ministries and give in the wrong places and also lose what we've earned due to those bad spiritual investments. The Israelites squandered their money, giving it unto blasphemies. Are we any better today? Entire ministries thrive, overtly false and misleading, and people pour their money into those ministries, watching their funds drain as if they put it in a bag pierced with many holes. God will blow away everything that is not of Him, as we watch it disappear. Watch where you spend your money, both leisurely and spiritually (Matthew 6:19-21, 2 Corinthians 4:7, 1 Timothy 6:19).

Haggai's words from God prove no matter how well we may seem to do on the outside, we are empty when we pursue things without God. Work can leave us void, food can leave us unsatisfied, alcohol can leave us without the comfort we seek, clothing can still reveal spiritual nakedness, and money can be spent on all the wrong things. Life is futile without solid, committed ministry. We need to see the church today in Haggai's words. In so many ways, we are so empty, sowing but not reaping, eating but not being filled, drinking but never drunk, wearing clothes but never warm, and earning wages that we lose as quickly as we gain them. The reality of our situation is we've pursued meaningless and selfish idols and ignored the Kingdom of God. How can we get back on track?

Haggai 1:7-11

This is what the LORD Almighty says: "Give careful thought to your ways. Go up into the mountains and bring down timber and build My house, so that I may take pleasure in it and be honored," says the LORD. "You expected much, but see, it turned out to be little. What you brought home, I blew away. Why?" declares the LORD Almighty. "Because of My house, which remains a ruin, while each of you is busy with your own house. Therefore, because of you the heavens have withheld their dew and the earth its crops. I called for a drought on the fields and the mountains, on the grain, the new wine, the olive oil and everything else the ground produces, on people and livestock, and on all the labor of your hands."

(Related Bible references: Exodus 29:45-46, Leviticus 26:19, Deuteronomy

28:23, Ruth 1:16-17, 2 Chronicles 6:26, 1 Kings 8:35, 1 Kings 17:1, 2 Kings 8:1, Job 38:1, Psalm 29:3, Song of Solomon 2:15, Jeremiah 3:3, Amos 1:2, Jeremiah 14:1-6, Matthew 13:1-20, Mark 4:1-20, Luke 8:4-15, Luke 12:26, Luke 16:10, Romans 5:2, Romans 11:5, Galatians 5:9, Ephesians 2:8, Galatians 6:8)

Once again, the Lord is calling Israel (and us) to carefully examine our ways. We need to think before we act and be deliberate in our Kingdom conduct.

Being a citizen of God's Kingdom is a deliberate action. We don't become citizens of any earthly nation without effort, and we don't become citizens of the Kingdom of God without effort, either. We must conform our ways unto His and align with the purpose and vision of the Kingdom of God. The first key to Kingdom citizenship is obedience.

Obedience is a big word loaded with a lot of meaning. As human beings, we like our autonomy. We like to be independent of everyone and everything else, forging our own way. We don't like instructions. When it comes to God, we like the idea that we can do what we like and God will remove any consequences for our failure to obey His word to us. As a result, obedience becomes a big issue for many in the Christian life. Theologians have debated for hundreds of years about the requirements of obedience for believers. Most of the answers we receive relate in extremes: either they say what we do is all that matters, or none of what we do matters. Both answers lack a display of true Scriptural understanding and Kingdom principle. As Christians, we recognize our salvation is only received by the grace of God through Jesus Christ our Lord (Romans 5:2, Romans 11:5, Ephesians 2:8). Thereafter, however, in that recognition, we should desire to align with God's precepts that point toward our transformation in Him. Repentance literally means to turn around and change our ways and follow the Lord's path. It is the beginning of a change, not the beginning of a new life doing the same things.

If we are to be a people of God's Kingdom, we are to be an obedient people, right down to the details of God's instruction. There is no specific task given to us that is too minute for us to obey. If little things can spoil what we do (Song of Solomon 2:15, Luke 12:26, Luke 16:10, Galatians 5:9), then little things also make a big difference.

God's instructions to the people were not just about making a temple; they were also a test of obedience. For sixteen years the Israelites lived completely preoccupied with their personal wants and ignored the priorities of God. The Israelites disobeyed God in other ways, as we can see from prophecies made in the same time frame, such as Nehemiah and Malachi. God's work with the Israelites in rebuilding the temple was a first step toward recapturing the necessary obedience for them to be His people, and He their God (Exodus 29:45-46, Ruth 1:16-17).

Haggai also raises an interesting point in the Lord's instructions: the people are to go, get the necessary materials, and build the Lord's house, that he may be honored therein. We first honor the Lord with our obedience and then honor Him with our praise and worship. Obedience must come first because it establishes a dwelling place for the Lord to live. He will not stay where He is not wanted. Through our obedience, we invite Him in; through our praise and worship, we welcome Him to stay and permanently dwell with and among us.

God also reveals much to us about the precept of sowing and reaping in this section of Haggai. The parable of the sower (Matthew 13:1-23, Mark 4:1-20, Luke 8:4-15) is often used in connection with evangelism. There's nothing wrong with understanding this interpretation, but we can also see something else in its contents: where we sow matters. Scattering seeds here, there, and everywhere, without dedicated purpose, won't produce results. Haggai also proves this through His prophecy. If we sow much without the Lord's blessing, sowing in areas that are contrary to His Kingdom, we will not reap the harvest we expect. We sow what we reap, and those who sow to destruction reap destruction (Galatians 6:8). We cannot randomly sow here and there, or sow anywhere other than where God has designated, and receive a harvest. If our Kingdom priorities are not established, we will not receive, no matter where we sow. We must tithe, offer, and provide for the ministry of God, that it may grow, if we want to see harvest in every area of our lives.

Where is the drought manifesting in our lives? We know God speaks through nature and weather patterns (Job 38:1, Psalm 29:3, Amos 1:2), but He also speaks to us about things in our lives through spiritual drought or spiritual harvest. Too often we attribute drought to the devil and gain to God. Sometimes God speaks to us as loudly through times that seem dry, distant, and dead as much as He does when things are good. If everything we touch seems to lead to negative results, we need to step back and seek God as to why that is. What is He telling us? Is the Kingdom of God first in our lives, or has something else become a priority? Are we being prepared for something else? What is most important to us? Answering these questions can direct us back to God and the obedience He requires, that He may dwell with us.

Haggai 1:12-15

Then Zerubbabel son of Shealtiel, Joshua son of Jozadak, the high priest, and the whole remnant of the people obeyed the voice of the LORD their God and the message of the prophet Haggai, because the LORD their God had sent him. And the people feared the LORD.

Then Haggai, the LORD's messenger, gave this message of the LORD to the people: "I am with you," declares the LORD. So the LORD stirred up the spirit of Zerubbabel son of Shealtiel, governor of Judah, and the spirit of Joshua son of Jozadak, the high priest, and the spirit of the whole remnant of the people. They came and began to work on the house of the LORD Almighty, their God, on the twenty-fourth day of the sixth month.

(Related Bible references: Genesis 1:26-28, Exodus 15:13, Exodus 25:2. Exodus 29:45, Leviticus 26:11, Leviticus 27:30-32, Numbers 18:21, Numbers 35:34, Deuteronomy 5:33, Deuteronomy 16:20, Deuteronomy 26:17, Deuteronomy 28:1-14, Deuteronomy 32:48-52, 2 Chronicles 36:22, Ezra 1:1, Ezra 5:2, Ezra 5:8, Job 34;12. Job 36:3, Psalm 8:1-9, Psalm 33:5, Psalm 36:6, Psalm 45:6, Psalm 62:11, Psalm 66:7, Psalm 103:6, Psalm 106:1, Psalm 110:3, Psalm 110:6, Psalm 111:10, Psalm 119:113, Psalm 145:9, Proverbs 1:7, Proverbs 16:6, Ecclesiastes 3:1-8Ecclesiastes 12:13, Isaiah 35:8, Isaiah 44:6, Isaiah 51:4, Isaiah 55:11, Jeremiah 7:23, Jeremiah 51:15, Nahum 1:7, Matthew 6:33, Matthew 9:6, Matthew 22:21, Matthew 28:20, Mark 12:17, Luke 1:3, Luke 1:68-75, Luke 20:25, John 4:24, Romans 1:16-17, Romans 6:16, Romans 6:19, Romans 8:29, Romans 8:31, Romans 13:1, 1 Corinthians 6:19, 1 Corinthians 12:28, 1 Corinthians 14:40, 1 Corinthians 15:58, 2 Corinthians 8:5, 2 Corinthians 8:19, 2 Corinthians 9:13, 2 Corinthians 10:6, Ephesians 2:4, 2 Timothy 3:5, Titus 1:5, James 1:8, James 2:23, James 4:8, 1 John 4:8, 1 John 4:16, Revelation 21:3)

Zerubbabel rises, along with the high priest and the people of Israel. They were stirred to obedience and recognized what they needed to do. They needed to turn away from themselves and return to the Lord and His work.

It must not have been easy to receive this correction. The people had to face themselves and realize they'd fallen into a common idolatry: the idolatry of self. They had to confront their own behavior, how they'd cast off the work of God in favor of catering to personal comforts. They had to accept that they had done wrong and make the situation right. It was a resolution of repentance, as they'd been on a certain course for a long time and needed to turn around and change to God's ways. This happened as a holy sense of fear and awe hit the Israelites thanks to God's prophecy.

This primary sense of fear and awe is essential to the believer, in both the repentance process and the continual sense of Kingdom awareness and obedience required of believers. It is not a reference to fear in the sense of anxiety or worry, but in the sense of holy reverence, true awe, and awareness of Who God is and the power He has. Reverential fear and awe truly reflect an understanding of God and a respect for His position in the universe (Psalm 8:1-9). Such an understanding makes us also aware of ourselves and our position in life. He is the Creator, and we are the created (Genesis 1:26-28). If we are to be an obedient people, unafraid and unashamed to bow before our God, we must be people that operate in fear and awe.

One of the reasons for the laxity in today's church is a detachment from fear and awe. We want God to be our buddy, our friend, someone with Whom we'd watch football or go shopping. Our understanding of God and His nature must be deeper than this. God is our Friend (James 2:23), but He is also our supreme authority figure (Psalm 62:11, Psalm 66:7, Matthew 9:6, Jeremiah 51:15). God's nature is love (Ephesians 2:4, 1 John 4:8, 1 John 4:16) and therefore is good (Psalm 106:1, Psalm 145:9, Nahum 1:7), but in love is also a sense of justice (Deuteronomy 16:20, Job 34:12, Job 36:3, Psalm 33:5, Psalm 36:6, Psalm 45:6, Psalm 103:6, Isaiah 51:4). Just because God is good doesn't mean that we walk into covenant with God free of expectations. If we have any understanding of God, that automatically demands our respect. He isn't another buddy whose opinion we seek every now and then; He is our Judge and Ruler (Psalm 110:6). If we maintain a sense of fear and awe, we will maintain a relationship with God based on obedience and truth.

God is with us when we remain focused on Him. It is God's purpose and will to establish a covenant people with which He may remain (Exodus 15:13, Exodus 29:45, Leviticus 26:11, Numbers 35:34, Revelation 21:3). How blessed to realize He is with us! He is with us when we are part of His Kingdom.

The first chapter of Haggai ends with a powerful conclusion. God stirred the spirit of the most unlikely candidate: the one sown in Babylon. Yet again we see the Lord's work advance through one that came out of the world, and into the Kingdom rather than one who was a part of God's people from the start. God knew Zerubbabel would never take for granted the Lord's presence in His life and would respond to God's prompting. The Lord stirred Zerubbabel's spirit, and Joshua the High Priest's spirit, that the people may be fully inspired and led. Following in order, the people also were stirred by the Father and followed the spiritual leading of the Lord as touched through their leaders. They got to work, repairing their Kingdom work, and attending to God's ministry once again. It was a new start, and a new direction, destination Kingdom. Such leadership facilitated the possibility and bond of unity within the community because they ascribed to God's divine order. When we truly understand the function and order of leaders within the church today, it too brings us to Christian unity.

It's important we hear this call today. As temples of the Holy Spirit (1 Corinthians 6:19), what is God calling you to do to rebuild His Kingdom ministry in this day and age? We are not in an age where we can say we'll do God's work later! It is time for us to step up and recognize the areas God calls us to make Kingdom priorities, and make them for ourselves:

- **Spiritual**: It truly amazes me the number of people who claim to be right with God, but in actuality are in total spiritual error. Many in the first century sought God for the things He could do for them, without loving Him for Who He is. In the current century, many still love God for what He can do for them, without loving Him for Who He is. It has remained a problem for centuries. God defines right spirituality as being in spirit and in truth (John 4:24). This means we must have more in our lives than spiritual motions, outward behaviors that resemble something spiritual, or the right Christian "look" without a true Kingdom mindset (2 Timothy 3:5). Being right with God spiritually means more than just having a relationship with God but having a right relationship with Him. It is a primary Kingdom responsibility to ensure we have a right relationship with our God in spirit and truth (doctrine, worship, teaching, understanding, and obedience).

- **Financial**: Many have distorted God's Word to make it unacceptable and uncomfortable for leaders to require their members bring forth tithes and offerings (Exodus 25:2, Leviticus 27:30-32, Numbers 18:21, 2 Corinthians 8:19). The numerous debates have caused many to justify themselves right out of giving to the work of God. Many will give, however, to every cause under the sun, every political cause, every thought group, and selfishly sow into their own desires, while neglecting God's work. I once heard a pastor point out that if as much money was poured into revival as is poured into politics, can we even imagine what would happen in the church! Financial giving is a part of Kingdom living. We don't expect to live as a citizen of any nation without paying taxes...so why do we assume Kingdom living comes without financial responsibility? As we give to Caesar what belongs to Caesar, we have no excuse or reason to ever forego giving unto God what belongs to Him (Matthew 22:21, Mark 12:17, Luke 20:25). If we have money for our entertainments, for the things we desire, for the things that often lure us most, for relationships, and for other things, then we have money for the Kingdom of God. Figuring out how to allocate resources is the necessary responsibility of every believer.

- **Lifestyle**: In keeping with Kingdom citizenship, we cannot do whatever we want and expect to reap Kingdom benefits. Our lives must speak the glory of God and point to Kingdom conduct and behavior. If we are not ascribing to God's standards of holiness (of being different for a spiritual purpose), we must step back and understand just how God asks us to live and follow Him in all we do in our everyday lives (Deuteronomy 32:48-52, Isaiah 35:8, Luke 1:68-75, Romans 6:19).

- **Time**: More and more people believe time with God is the one acceptable area of life to "cut" down when time is needed for other activities. We never see others cut out their entertainment, jobs, families, leisure activities, or other areas; only time with God. People are impatient with church services that run longer than anticipated and frustrated when God asks things of them which they don't want to do. Where is God in your time? Have you become so busy with so many things that you can't make a full commitment to any area God calls you to answer? We learn in God's Word there is a time for everything (Ecclesiastes 3:1-8). That means there is time for God! Stop cutting God's time because you don't want to fully commit yourself to the Kingdom!

- **Commitment**: The world today is extremely fast-paced and multi-faceted. Most jobs consider "multi-tasking" a plus to job performance. In a certain sense, the ability to do more than one thing at a time is a gift. In a deeper sense, multi-tasking causes a lack of choices and confusion about commitment in an individual. If all of us are so busy pursuing many things at once, we are not making the choice about how we will use our time and what commitments we will make to certain things. In the Kingdom, we are faced with constant choices and decisions about what we will do, how we will glorify God, and how making different choices will affect our commitment to God. If we are to seek first the Kingdom of God and His righteousness (Matthew 6:33), that means our first commitment is to God – not our families, not our jobs, not our selfish interests, and not what we want. We prioritize around God's precepts and Kingdom beliefs, not make commitments the other way around (Isaiah 44:6, Romans 8:29, 2 Corinthians 8:5).

- **Obedience**: How is your obedience to God? It's not uncommon to try and sidestep what God tells us to do because it isn't something we want to do, like to do, or because we find it inconvenient. When we are obedient, we do what God says: we meet His requirements to us as a group, we meet His requirements to us as individuals, and we do what He instructs us to do directly. Obedience is a lifestyle whereby we respect the fullness of His commands to us in every area of our lives, without fail, even when it's inconvenient or hard (Deuteronomy 5:33, Deuteronomy 26:17, Deuteronomy 28:1-14, Jeremiah 7:23, Romans 6:16, 2 Corinthians 9:13, 2 Corinthians 10:6).

- **Integrity**: It's been said that "Integrity means doing the right thing, even when no one is looking." How consistent are we in our character? As Kingdom citizens, we can't do one thing at one time and then do something different another time (Psalm 119:113, James 1:8, James 4:8). We must be individuals who are consistent in our behavior, upholding the same standards and expecting others to maintain certain consistent ethics in their dealings with us. We cannot be controlled or swayed by feelings, false doctrine, or false influences (Matthew 22:16).

- **Order**: The church today is highly resistant to the order of God (Romans 13:1, 1 Corinthians 12:28, Titus 1:5). Today's people want to be obedient and follow after those leaders who cater to their tastes rather than submitting themselves to the leadership God has established. God's order is far beyond submission to leadership, however; it is submitting to God's system and method of conveying information, of obedience and discipline, and His path for us in life (Luke 1:3, Romans 1:16-17, 1 Corinthians 14:40). Order is the method by which God's people walk in His disciplines with the end of becoming self-disciplined people, representing the Lord in all their doings.

We can speak about the church's state today in general terms, comparing us to the Israelites of Haggai's day. There's nothing wrong in doing so, but at the end of the day, we must examine ourselves if we want things to change. It's easy to look around and feel the problem is another Christian, another believer, another person whose priorities are messy. Where are your futility levels as you study this first chapter of Haggai?

It's very possible you struggle in one – or more than one – of the areas we've examine in this chapter. This is your moment, your time to discern how God calls you to change and focus more on the rebuilding of His temple within you.

r meis labium electum ut inuocet oms i nole
ram 7 seruiant ei humero uno ult flumina eti-
cel mei filij dispsor meoz deferent munt i
illa ñ cõfundis te cunctis adinuentõib; tuis q
 prancata el m me qa tc auferam de medio
magniloquos sbie tue ñ adiciet exaltari ã
ul m monte sco meo 7 delinqä m medio tui po
lum paupem 7 egenum 7 spabunt m nole dñi re
uie dñi· non facient iniquitatem nec loquetur
dacum 7 ñ inuenietur m ore eoz lingua dolo
osu qr ipsi pascentur 7 accubabunt cu erit equer
t h dicit dominus lauda filia syon iubila filia
im letare 7 exulta isrł m omni corde filia ierłm
tulit dñs iudicium tuum auertit inimicos tuos
e isrł dñs m medio tui ñ timeb malum ultra m
illa dicet ierłm noli timere syon ñ dissoluantur
manus tue· dñs deus tuus m medio tui fortis ipe sal
bit gaudebit sup te m letitia silebit m dilectõe su
cultabit sup te m laude· nugas qui alege· recesse
et cõggabo qr ex te erant 7 ñ habeas ultra sup eis
pbrium· ecce ego interficiam oms hi laeserint te
flicient te m tempore illo 7 saluabo claudicans
m 7 eam q erecta fuit cõggabo 7 ponam eos
laudem 7 m nomen 7 omni terra confusionis eoz
z illo euo adducam uos 7 m tpe euo cõggabo
os dabo enim uos m nomen 7 m laudem oib;

rpt restauratoil ierłm aduen
credulitatem ipłi uellent tpe
per eum· ipłi hre diē ñ dum te
domus dei omnia q q uerci hu
reułicoem ipłi edificarent tem
ret obsuantiam sacerdotalem
eoz significant incipit agg.

n anno scdo darij regis psau
ac scm est uerbum domini m ma
ypbabel filium salatihel duce
iosedech sacerdotem magnum
eum dicens ipłe ide dit
dñi edificandos scm est uerbum
ypłe dicens sic dit tps uob e
scaris· domus ista destruct
surate corda ura scd uias ura
tulistis parum comedistis opu
eum mercedes cõggauit
prusum sed dicit dominus ed
ura scd uias uras ascendite
ea 7 edificate domum 7 acce
cabor dixit dominus respe
scm e minus 7 inculistis m do
quam ob cam dit dñs ex
debra e 7 uos festinatit m

CHAPTER TWO

A CHOSEN REMNANT AND A CHOSEN PERSON FOR A CHOSEN TIME (HAGGAI CHAPTER 2)

Key verses

- **Verses 3-4**: *'Who of you is left who saw this house in its former glory? How does it look to you now? Does it not seem to you like nothing? But now be strong, Zerubbabel,' declares the LORD. 'Be strong, Joshua son of Jozadak, the high priest. Be strong, all you people of the land,' declares the LORD, 'and work. For I am with you,' declares the LORD Almighty.*

- **Verses 6-7**: *"This is what the LORD Almighty says: 'In a little while I will once more shake the heavens and the earth, the sea and the dry land. I will shake all nations, and what is desired by all nations will come, and I will fill this house with glory,' says the LORD Almighty.*

- **Verse 8-9**: *'The silver is Mine and the gold is Mine,' declares the LORD Almighty. 'The glory of this present house will be greater than the glory of the former house,' says the LORD*

Almighty. 'And in this place I will grant peace,' declares the LORD Almighty."

- **Verses 13-14:** *Then Haggai said, "If a person defiled by contact with a dead body touches one of these things, does it become defiled?" "Yes," the priests replied, "it becomes defiled." Then Haggai said, "'So it is with this people and this nation in my sight,' declares the LORD. Whatever they do and whatever they offer there is defiled.*

- **Verses 17-19:** *'From this day on, from this twenty-fourth day of the ninth month, give careful thought to the day when the foundation of the LORD's temple was laid. Give careful thought: Is there yet any seed left in the barn? Until now, the vine and the fig tree, the pomegranate and the olive tree have not borne fruit. "'From this day on I will bless you.'"*

Words and phrases to know

- **Remnant:** From the Hebrew word *she'eriyth* which means "rest, residue, remainder, remnant."[1]

- **Glory:** From the Hebrew word *kabowd* which means "glory, honor, glorious, abundance."[2]

- **Look:** From the Hebrew word *ra'ah* which means "to see, look at, inspect, perceive, consider."[3]

- **Be strong:** From the Hebrew word *chazaq* which means "to strengthen, prevail, harden, be strong, become strong, be courageous, be firm, grow firm, be resolute, grow sore."[4]

- **Covenanted:** From the Hebrew word *karath* which means "to cut, cut off, cut down, cut off a body part, cut out, eliminate, kill, cut a covenant."[5]

- **Spirit:** From the Hebrew word *ruwach'* which means "wind, breath, mind, spirit."[6]

- **Do not fear**: From the Hebrew word *yare'* which means "to fear, revere, be afraid; to shoot, pour."[7]

- **Shake**: From the Hebrew word *ra'ash* which means "to quake, shake."[8]

- **Sea**: From the Hebrew word *yam* which means "sea."[9]

- **Dry land**: From the Hebrew word *charabah* which means "dry land, dry ground."[10]

- **All nations**: From the Hebrew word *gowy* which means "nation, people."[11]

- **Desired**: From the Hebrew word *chemdah* which means "desire, that which is desirable; pleasant, precious."[12]

- **Come**: From the Hebrew word *bow'* which means "to go in, enter, come, go, come in."[13]

- **Silver**: From the Hebrew word *keceph* which means "silver, money."[14]

- **Gold**: From the Hebrew word *zahab* which means "gold."[15]

- **Present**: From the Hebrew word *'acharown* which means "behind, following, subsequent, western."[16]

- **Former**: From the Hebrew word *ri'shown* which means "first, primary, former; first, before, formerly, at first."[17]

- **Peace**: From the Hebrew word *shalowm* which means "completeness, soundness, welfare, peace."[18]

- **Priests**: From the Hebrew word *kohen* which means "priest, principal officer or chief ruler."[19]

- **Law**: From the Hebrew word *towrah* which means "law, direction, instruction."[20]

- **Consecrated meat**: From two Hebrew words: *quodesh* which means "apartness, holiness, sacredness, separateness;"[22] and *basar* which means "flesh."[23]

- **Fold of their garment**: From the Hebrew word *shaphal* which means "low, humble."[24]

- **Defiled**: From the Hebrew word *tame'* which means "unclean, impure."[25]

- **Offer**: From the Hebrew word *qarab* which means "to approach, enter into, draw near."[26]

- **Stone**: From the Hebrew word *'eben* which means "stone (large or small)."[27]

- **Temple**: From the Hebrew word *heykal* which means "palace, temple, nave, sanctuary."[28]

- **Struck**: From the Hebrew word *nakah* which means "to strike, smite, hit, beat, slay, kill."[29]

- **Blight**: From the Hebrew word *shedephah* which means "blighted or blasted thing, blighted, blasted; blight (of crops)."[30]

- **Mildew**: From the Hebrew word *yeraqown* which means "mildew, paleness, lividness."[31]

- **Hail**: From the Hebrew word *barad* which means "to hail."[32]

- **Overturn**: From the Hebrew word *haphak* which means "to turn, overthrow, overturn."[33]

- **Royal thrones**: From two Hebrew words: *kicce'* which means "seat (of honor), throne, seat, stool;"[34] and *mamlakah* which means "kingdom, domain, reign, sovereignty."[35]

- **Power**: From the Hebrew word *chozeq* which means "strength."[36]

- **By the sword of his own brother**: From two Hebrew words: *chereb* which means "sword, knife;"[37] and *'ach* which means "brother."[38]

- **Servant**: From the Hebrew word *'ebed* which means "slave, servant."[39]

- **Signet ring**: From the Hebrew word *chowtham* which means "seal, signet, signet-ring."[40]

- **Chosen**: From the Hebrew word *bachar* which means "to choose, elect, decide for."[41]

Haggai 2:1-5

On the twenty-first day of the seventh month, the word of the LORD came through the prophet Haggai: "Speak to Zerubbabel son of Shealtiel, governor of Judah, to Joshua son of Jozadak, the high priest, and to the remnant of the people. Ask them, 'Who of you is left who saw this house in its former glory? How does it look to you now? Does it not seem to you like nothing? But now be strong, Zerubbabel,' declares the LORD. 'Be strong, Joshua son of Jozadak, the high priest. Be strong, all you people of the land,' declares the LORD, 'and work. For I am with you,' declares the LORD Almighty. 'This is what I covenanted with you when you came out of Egypt. And My Spirit remains among you. Do not fear.'

[Related Bible references: Exodus 10:7, Exodus 16:18, Exodus 29:45, Exodus 34:17, Leviticus 19:4, Leviticus 26:1, Deuteronomy 4:29, Deuteronomy 6:5, Deuteronomy 11:1, Deuteronomy 12:5, Deuteronomy 28:20, Deuteronomy 28:63, Joshua 1:9, 2 Samuel 10:12, 1 Chronicles 16:26, 2 Chronicles 6:14, 2

Chronicles 14:4, Psalm 37:4, Psalm 103:5, Psalm 105:24, Psalm 122:9. Psalm 145;16, Psalm 145;19, Proverbs 10:14, Ecclesiastes 4:5, Isaiah 2:8, Isaiah 3:10, Isaiah 7:14, Isaiah 41:6, Isaiah 53:1-12, Isaiah 58:10-11, Isaiah 63:11, Lamentations 3:47, Ezekiel 5:14, Ezra 3:12, Nehemiah 9:20, Hosea 4:12, Jonah 2:8, Micah 6:3, Micah 6:16, Zechariah 4:10, Zechariah 8:9, Zechariah 8:13, Matthew 1:23, Matthew 3:8-10, Matthew 6:8, Matthew 6:32-33, Matthew 7:16-20, Matthew 12:33, Matthew 19:26, Matthew 21:43, Mark 10:27, Luke 6:43-44, Luke 17:21-22, John 14:6, John 3:30, John 15:4, Acts 17:6, Acts 17:27, Romans 3:16-17, Romans 8:26, Romans 8:31, Romans 12:3-8, 1 Corinthians 5;11, 1 Corinthians 6:9, 1 Corinthians 6:19, 1 Corinthians 12:1-11, 1 Corinthians 15:43, 2 Corinthians 9:8, 2 Corinthians 12:9-10, Galatians 5:22, Ephesians 4:7-16, Hebrews 4:16, Hebrews 11:4-40, 2 Peter 1:3, 1 John 5:21)

Haggai chapter 2 opens in a similar style to Haggai chapter 1. The word of God came forth through Haggai the prophet unto Zerubbabel, Joshua the high priest, and the people of Israel. Unlike the beginning of Haggai chapter 1, the people of Israel already received their emphatic and intense command to rebuild the temple. The people had already received their stern scolding for living without Kingdom priorities for several years and were set and established to now focus on God's Kingdom ministry.

The first thing we can recognize in Haggai 2 is the people of Israel are referred to as a "remnant." There are two notable things in their label as a "remnant." The first key is that, as a remnant, they were only a returning fraction of the original number who went into captivity. The majority of Israel never made it out of their captivity. This returning group was specifically called by God to restore the glory of the temple and restore His presence among His people. In keeping with this theme, the second notable facet is given in God's indication of numbers. The remnant of Israel was more than capable to do the work of temple rebuilding and Kingdom restoration.

So often Christians think the biggest churches and ministries are the ones doing things correctly. They assume that having the most money, the most people, and getting the most notoriety equates to having the best church. While the work of God knows no limit, it is far more reasonable to question where those big churches and ministries started out. Every true Kingdom building starts out with a "remnant," a small fraction of the larger body. In many instances, that remnant stands in total opposition to what those around them are doing. The work of the remnant serves three basic purposes:

- **Prove the work is of God, and not of human beings**: A small, committed remnant proves the power of God surpasses human abilities. What may seem impossible in the natural-by-natural vision and sight is totally possible with God, because all things are possible with Him (Matthew 19:26, Mark 10:27). It's not a miracle for something to happen with a million people...but it's definitely a miracle for something to happen when you impact a million lives with only a handful of people. Never doubt it's possible...this is the very definition of salvation history!

- **Prove God's work is about spiritual strength, not numbers**: The world teaches there is strength in numbers. In the Kingdom, we see the entire world turned upside down by a handful of apostles (Acts 17:6), not to mention the many other instances of change and empowerment brought about by a small number of people (Hebrews 11:4-40). A remnant has the power to change the world!

  In connection with this reality, we are drawn to the fact that throughout salvation history, God has always only had a remnant. God has never worked through the largest group of people, but always the smallest. Even within that scope, there has always been a remnant within God's numbers who've gotten the job done.

- **Explore the essential aspects of spiritual dedication and obedience to God**: God deals with remnants because He can better teach and direct them. The relationship which develops between a remnant and God is stronger, more personal, and more telling for obedience than with a larger group.

Remnant people are called to rebuild something torn down, done away with, ignored, or forsaken by a larger group. This is both a monumental task and also one that must be understood. The people of God did not understand their position as God's remnant people. Still living with captivity mentality meant the people didn't see the full ramifications of their behavior in ignoring Kingdom priorities. We can clearly see the confusion of the people on essential Kingdom matters. The mere fact that they allowed the temple to lie in ruin and temple service to cease for so many years reveals their lack of true revelation on Kingdom citizenship. Given the 16 years that had passed since they'd returned from captivity, the ramifications of such Kingdom neglect are staggering. Those young or born around the time of the return were now adults and had never lived with the precept of Kingdom ministry as a priority. Older ones had forgotten, while younger ones never knew the truth. Even though they'd received the command to rebuild, the people of Israel needed to see the state of the temple, face-to-face, to recognize their own state. It was by their own choice and neglect that the temple was in its truly unspeakable state. What had happened within them to allow God's ministry to sit in ruin?

The people of Israel forgot God. In their own pain and misery of captivity, they began to think only of themselves. Their focus was on what they had to give up...what they had to sacrifice...what they had lost...what they were missing out on...what they wanted...what they were going through...their focus was themselves. They only sought God's restitution what they felt they'd lost. It was about things, not spirituality. Their ministry was exclusively the care and desires of themselves. In such a state, God is not a focus.

Many of us believe that believing in God automatically equates to a right relationship with God. People can believe in God, believe God provides, and even believe God to meet their desires and still have a wrong relationship with Him. Like any relationship, our relationship with God can be functional or dysfunctional. Recognizing this fact helps us assess ourselves more completely in our spiritual state and come to see facts rather than feelings in our perspectives of the divine.

Many in Christianity have a dysfunctional relationship with God, as they do not know Him as they should. They see God as a Santa Claus figure, One Who should provide them every want without consideration for ever learning more of Who He is. I once heard it described that there's a difference between seeking the glory of God and the presence of God. If we attempt to seek one without the other, all we have is a hobby. In language used here, we have a dysfunctional relationship by which we expect God to perform on whim, constantly proving He is God to us.

God isn't insecure and has no need to constantly prove He is God to humanity...especially when we have plenty of evidence to know Who He is for ourselves. Seeking God for everything is not a sign that someone is truly where they need to be in their relationship with God. While we are to seek God for our needs (Exodus 16:18, Isaiah 58:10-11, Matthew 6:8, Matthew 6:32, 2 Corinthians 9:8, Hebrews 4:16, 2 Peter 1:3) and Scripture tells us He will give us the desires of our heart (Psalm 37:4, Psalm 103:5, Psalm 122:9. Psalm 145:16, Psalm 145:19), we are also to have a deeper relationship with God than mere give and take. Having a relationship with God indicates we desire to know more about God and spend time with God. We must come to read about Him in His word, spend time with Him in prayer, operate in worship and praise, and desire to know more about Him. We should never believe we've seen enough of God, have enough of Him, or have no more room for the Lord. In keeping with the principle of relationship, our true desire in life should be to spend time with and love the Lord.

In keeping with the principle of relationship, relationships do not just reveal to us truths about others; they also reveal truths about ourselves. When one is in a relationship with another person long-term, that relationship reveals areas of needed growth, change, and enhancement. A true relationship with God does just this: it reveals us, uncovering areas where we must decrease, and He must increase (John 3:30). We should never, ever assume we are perfect with God. Believing in God and having a relationship with Him should never, ever serve as an excuse to ignore character flaws or areas of personal growth.

The ruined temple of God represented the relationship God had with Israel. Its broken-down, neglected state reflected where they were with God as individuals. Even though they seemed to have the best of everything, they had nothing, because they did not have God. Each Israelite needed to see themselves in that damaged, ruined temple. To restore, they had to recognize, through their relationship with God, where they truly were.

There are many ways in which we can assess our relationship with God and see our state face-to-face. As temples of the Holy Ghost, we are now God's living temple (1 Corinthians 6:19). It's easy for us to look around at our churches, our mirror reflections as we stand well-dressed in fancy suits, and the things we have. If we assess ourselves by nothing else, we won't find what we need revealed. How can we know where we truly are in our relationship with God? Here are some important, indicating factors:

- **How much time do I spend with the Lord?**: Time spent with the Lord must go beyond a weekly church obligation. It must also go beyond a "have-to" kind of mentality where one sets a legalistic attitude to Scripture reading, prayer, worship, praise, and devotionals. Just getting through time with God means we are just getting through our relationship with Him. Our time with God prepares us for the times when life isn't so focused and quiet, so we can dialogue with the Lord in any and every situation (Deuteronomy 4:29, Deuteronomy 12:5, 2 Chronicles 14:4, Acts 17:27, Hebrews 11:6). In keeping with the personal nature of our relationship with God, we must find our time with God to speak to us as loudly as anyone dictating our relationship with Him. Whatever form our spiritual time forms our ability to hear from God is how we find God.

- **Is the "ministry" God calling me to in a state of ruin?**: God calls every one of us to do something in this world. Not everyone will be called to full-time, five-fold church ministry, but everyone will be called to do a work for God, their established ministry in their lives. Whether it's preaching, running a business, working as a nurse, being a great teacher, or anything else one may be called to do, it's essential to step back every now and then and take "inventory." Are people responding to what God has called you to do? While some are called to have larger followings in work than others, a constant state of revolving people, complaints about conduct or questions about integrity, and constant "head-butting" with others should cause us to step back and do some serious personal assessment. Where is God's appointed ministry in us? If we are in ruin, we need to figure out why (Exodus 10:7, Deuteronomy 28:20, Deuteronomy 28:63, Proverbs 10:14, Ecclesiastes 4:5, Lamentations 3:47, Ezekiel 5:14, Micah 6:3, Micah 6:16, Romans 3:16-17).

- **What is the most important thing in my life?**: Some people say it's their family, some people say it's their spouse, some people say it's their job...what is the most important thing in your life? If you are a true believer living in God's Kingdom, your answer as to what is the most important thing in your life should be nothing but God. Anything else but God, in this instance, is an idol, as it's coming before Him in your life. If there's anything that is coming first – even under the guise of seeking it from God or thinking God wants you to have it – it's time to lay that aside and seek God (Exodus 34:17, Leviticus 19:4, Leviticus 26:1, Deuteronomy 6:5, Deuteronomy 11:1, 1 Chronicles 16:26, 2 Chronicles 6:14, Isaiah 2:8, Hosea 4:12, Jonah 2:8, Matthew 6:33, 1 Corinthians 5;11, 1 Corinthians 6:9, 1 John 5:21).

- **What kind of "fruit" does my life display?**: Sometimes we think we are stronger in our relationship with God than we, in actuality, are. We mistake certain things – such as getting something we want or a situation working out to our advantage – as signs we are in God's will, while ignoring serious signals we are not right in our relationship with God. How well do we get along with others? Are we obedient with God and in alignment with His conducts for holiness? Have we attempted to "pick and choose" what aspects of His guidelines we find most desirable, while ignoring the rest? Do we feel entitled to receive from God? Do we have certain attitudes about faith and God that hamper our witness or behavior? Our best indication of our relationship with God is the fruit we bear. If we aren't bearing any fruit or the right fruit...odds are good we are not right with Him (Psalm 105:24, Isaiah 3:10, Matthew 3:8-10, Matthew 7:16-20,

Matthew 12:33, Matthew 19:26, Matthew 21:43, Mark 10:27, Luke 6:43-44, John 15:4, Galatians 5:22).

Through the temple, God provided this sobering, life-altering encounter with self to the people of Israel. If they were going to resume ministry, it needed to be done right. We just can't pick up anywhere and hope God will bless our efforts. The temple represents us before we are born again, whenever we are far from God, or in a broken state before Him. We start with humble selves and God builds within us, establishing His Kingdom first within, and then among (Luke 17:21-22).

Given this fact, it's no wonder the Lord commands Zerubbabel, Joshua, and all the people of the land to be strong! The process to build the ministry of God is not an easy one. It takes personal commitment and dedication as well as dedication among leadership and the remnant group. Remnants do the job of a much larger body. To accomplish this, they must completely and totally rely on the Lord. We must prepare ourselves for every possible complication and rest in God's love and mercy. In our weaknesses, He will strengthen us (Romans 8:26, 1 Corinthians 15:43, 2 Corinthians 12:9-10), and where we can be even stronger, God will strengthen us (Joshua 1:9, 2 Samuel 10:12, Isaiah 41:6, Zechariah 8:13).

Verse 4 reveals the reason why we can be strong: God is with us. Do we consider what it means to have God with us? God's promise to be with us, as we abide by His precepts, is His basic covenantal promise, dating all the way back to when the Israelites departed from Egypt. Jesus Christ was Emmanuel, which means, "God with us" (Isaiah 7:14, Matthew 1:23). Through Jesus Christ, we recognize God living within us and working for us. It was as result of His sacrifice that the way was made for us to come fully unto the Father (Isaiah 53:1-12. John 14:6). Through Christ, we receive the Holy Spirit, God alive, living and active, and with us in our experience today. God's presence in our lives can never be understated! As God works with us and within us, all things are truly possible (Matthew 19:26, Mark 10:27).

As we are His people, attending to His work, we have nothing to fear. His Spirit is with us, alive and active, and we can see God work through His spiritual gifts given to us (Romans 12:3-8, 1 Corinthians

12:1-11, Ephesians 4:7-16). Considering the Almighty Creator's great work, His call unto us is certainly nothing to fear!

Most relevant, God reveals the reason why we are strong: so we can work. We are not equipped with strength so we can feel good about ourselves, be lazy, or lag around, waiting for something to happen. God infuses our strength so we can work, move forward with matters, and stand without fear in His purpose. We are called to not just be strong...but be strong and work.

Haggai 2:6-9

"This is what the LORD Almighty says: 'In a little while I will once more shake the heavens and the earth, the sea and the dry land. I will shake all nations, and what is desired by all nations will come, and I will fill this house with glory,' says the LORD Almighty. 'The silver is mine and the gold is mine,' declares the LORD Almighty. 'The glory of this present house will be greater than the glory of the former house,' says the LORD Almighty. 'And in this place I will grant peace,' declares the LORD Almighty."

(Related Bible references: Genesis 3:15. Genesis 22:18, Genesis 49:10, Exodus 25:1-40, Exodus 26:1-37, Leviticus 27:30-32, Deuteronomy 4:12, Deuteronomy 12:6, Deuteronomy 14:24-25, Deuteronomy 18:15, Psalm 24:7, Psalm 29:3, Psalm 29:7-9, Psalm 85:8-9. Psalm 149:9, Isaiah 9:6. Isaiah 24:4-6, Isaiah 26:3, Isaiah 52:7, Isaiah 54:3, Isaiah 55:12, Daniel 7:18-22, Joel 2:30-32, Joel 3:16, Malachi 3:1, Malachi 3:10, Matthew 3:2, Matthew 5:9, Matthew 24:30-41, Mark 1:15, Mark 4:22, Mark 13:24-25, Mark 17:34-35, Luke 2:14, Luke 6:38, Luke 8:17, Luke 11:31, Luke 12:2, Luke 13:3, John 1:14, John 14:27, Romans 12:18, 1 Corinthians 6:2, 2 Corinthians 9:7, Ephesians 2:14, Ephesians 4:7-16, Acts 1:10-11, Acts 2:21, Acts 2:38, Acts 3:19, Hebrews 12:26-28, 2 Peter 3:8-13, Jude 1:14-15, Revelation 6:12-14, Revelation 8:5-13, Revelation 11:15, Revelation 21:9-26, Revelation 22:12-21)

God's prophetic shift in verse 6 is most interesting. The entire first chapter of Haggai, and the first five verses of Haggai chapter 2, all point to Israel's realities about themselves, what they had done to God's ministry, and the command to rebuild ministry and start again. Now God shifts to future prophetic events, letting His people know events to come, that they may prepare in kind for what is to come.

In reality, God's entire call to His remnant people had the

purpose of preparing for what was to come. Remnants are called for a specific purpose: to prepare for something and build because a paradigm shift is approaching. God's Kingdom call: to repent, for the Kingdom of heaven is at hand (Matthew 3:2, Mark 1:15, Luke 13:3, Acts 2:38, Acts 3:19) and call upon the Name of the Lord (Joel 2:32, Acts 2:21) tells us those who are alive in God's Kingdom today are a remnant people. We must attend to the ministry of God because another paradigm shift is coming. We must know and identify this paradigm shift, passing from the kingdoms of this world to the full central implementation of the Kingdom of God (Hebrews 12:28, Revelation 11:15).

God's prophetic word in Haggai 2:6-9 applies to both the first coming of Christ and the second coming of Christ. The remnant of Israel needed to restore ministry in preparation for Christ's first advent. Today, we need to restore God's full ministry in preparation of Christ's second advent. How do we prepare for Jesus' return? We know we must prepare ourselves, but how do we prepare the church? The answer lies in God's prophecy of what is to come:

- **See ourselves in the prophecy**: The literal, physical temple prophesied in this passage was later destroyed. While it might have held glory for a time, this passage applies to both the believer before and after salvation (former and latter glory), passing from death to life and becoming the temple of the Holy Spirit, and the church passing from a broken state to the glorified Bride of Christ.

- **The heavens and the earth will be shaken = We must prepare and warn of literal shifts in the physical earth's state of being and changes to come (Isaiah 24:4-6, Joel 2:30, Mark 13:24-25, 2 Peter 3:8-13, Revelation 6:12-14, Revelation 8:5-13)**: Natural disturbances are a key element of last days prophecy. We must recognize these signs so we can understand prophecy and rightly interpret it. In these natural disasters lie a key of God's voice in this day and age and His message to humanity (Deuteronomy 4:12, Psalm 29:3, Psalm 29:7-9). If we are to give people key insight into

God's word for today, we must understand and recognize natural signs of the times.

- **All nations will be shaken = The church must prepare itself to fully accept its governmental seat as God's ruling establishment (Psalm 149:9, Daniel 7:18-22, 1 Corinthians 6:2, Jude 1:14-15)**: The nations of this earth exist by ordered conspiracy. In the last days, God uncovers all covered things (Mark 4:22, Luke 8:17, Luke 12:2) and breaks up established conspiracies (Matthew 24:36-41, Mark 17:34-35) in the preparation of restoring order. Things social, political, and cultural will be disturbed, upset, moved, switched, and ultimately destroyed or changed. It is so essential the Kingdom ministry stands assembled and prepared because God's Kingdom government shall take the place of errant and ruling governors when Jesus returns (Psalm 149:9, Daniel 7:18-22, 1 Corinthians 6:2, Jude 1:14-15). This means the church must be active in the restoration of the five-fold ministry, God's established Kingdom government, for this approaching time (Ephesians 4:7-16).

- **The Desire of All Nations shall come = The second coming of Jesus Christ (Matthew 24:30-35, Acts 1:10-11, Revelation 22:12-21)**: The world has numerous desires, but only one Desire. In this day and age, much like in the days of Haggai, the world chases after its many desires, rather than the true Desire. It is our prophetic place to stand as people who seek Jesus Christ, the Desire of all nations, Who truly is the answer to all we seek (Malachi 3:1).

- **The present glory of this house (ministry) will not compare to the future glory = Preparation for the Bride of Christ, the church, to meet with Christ, and rule with Him (Psalm 149:9, Daniel 7:18-22, 1 Corinthians 6:2, Jude 1:14-15)**: Ministry today is both a reality and a type. We are the Kingdom of God, living and active upon this earth (Revelation 21:9, Revelation 22:17). We are also a shadow of all that will come in ministry in the future, after Christ returns. The glory of the

51

church, present in varying degrees all throughout history, is nothing to be compared with the incredible glory and splendor that awaits us at His return (Psalm 149:9, Daniel 7:18-22, 1 Corinthians 6:2, Jude 1:14-15, Revelation 21:9, Revelation 22:17).

- **The silver and gold belong to God = Our Kingdom priority is expressed financially, through giving tithes and offerings (Leviticus 27:30-32, Deuteronomy 12:6, Deuteronomy 14:24-25, Malachi 3:10, Luke 6:38, 2 Corinthians 9:7)**: Money is a sticky subject in today's church. There are many in the church who are greedy. At the same time, there are many in the church who have unmet needs because others are greedy. Our position of clear extremes has erased the power of balance on this essential issue. Today's church has made money issues confusing, taboo, and unspeakable. It's impossible to teach on God's precepts about finances without being accused of being greedy, money-oriented, or in ministry for the wrong reasons. What many forget in the vein of giving to God's ministry is we are simply returning a portion of what already belongs to Him. Using these natural elements, God will bring glory and splendor to the New Jerusalem after Christ returns (Revelation 21:9-26). We also recognize silver and gold were used in the ancient temple (Exodus 25:1-40, Exodus 26:1-37), as types of perfect redemption and purification. In giving of our silver and gold to God, we are also recognizing our perfect redemption and purification comes from Him.

- **In this place, God will grant peace = The Millennial reign of Christ arrives with peace, and as peaceful people, we walk in anticipation of this day (Isaiah 26:3, Isaiah 52:7, Matthew 5:9, Romans 12:18)**: Scripture repeatedly emphasizes the importance of peace, being a peaceful people, bringing peace to situations, and standing as a people who are not moved with every wind that blows through the world. Peace is the ability to bring stability into any situation, emotion, or problem. It doesn't mean the storm ceases, but that the storm ceases within us and those who receive God's peace (Isaiah 26:3, Isaiah 52:7, John 14:27). This peace is a type of existence that shall be permanent in the day Jesus returns and restores all things to peace and order (Isaiah 54:3, Isaiah 55:12, 2 Peter 3:11-13).

There is no question from the above that restoration brings blessing. Restoration is the ultimate type of God's true restoring nature. By His grace and power, He can transform the hearts of lost and fallen men and make sinners into saints. Restoration also bears responsibility, as restoration is a process. God calls His remnant people to bring about restoration and stand as that sign of restoration to the world, showing others there are better things ahead and the time is growing near for such things to happen. Battered and tired, worn and weary from the world, God's remnant people prove restoration exists, it is more than possible, and totally accessible. The people themselves are a type, a sign, a pointing, and a shadow of the promise to come, and God's prophecy to be fulfilled. What a privilege to take our place in prophecy as His modern-day remnant!

Haggai 2:10-14

On the twenty-fourth day of the ninth month, in the second year of Darius, the word of the LORD came to the prophet Haggai: "This is what the LORD Almighty says: 'Ask the priests what the law says: If someone carries consecrated meat in the fold of their garment, and that fold touches some bread or stew, some wine, olive oil or other food, does it become consecrated?'"

The priests answered, "No."

Then Haggai said, "If a person defiled by contact with a dead body touches one of these things, does it become defiled?"

"Yes," the priests replied, "it becomes defiled."

Then Haggai said, "'So it is with this people and this nation in My sight,' declares the LORD. 'Whatever they do and whatever they offer there is defiled.

(Related Bible references: Leviticus 10:1-20, Leviticus 18:24, Numbers 19:11,

Deuteronomy 4:2, Deuteronomy 4:39, Deuteronomy 6:6, Deuteronomy 10:16, Deuteronomy 12:32, Deuteronomy 28:1-14, Deuteronomy 33:10, Proverbs 4:23, Jeremiah 2:7, Jeremiah 3:9, Jeremiah 4:18, Jeremiah 6:15, Jeremiah 32:34, Malachi 2:7, Mark 3:29, Acts 7:51, 1 Corinthians 8:7, Ephesians 2:1-22, Ephesians 4:17, Ephesians 4:30, Philippians 4:4-9, 2 Thessalonians 2:13, Titus 1:15, Hebrews 12:15, 1 Peter 2:5, 2 Peter 3:1)

God just proclaimed great words over Israel. They were to be a part of preparation for God's coming paradigm shift! He spoke to them a word of hope and life in verses 6-9, depicting what He would do and why their remnant work was so essential. Now, starting in verse 10, God has switched back to the issue of where they are right now. In receiving the promise and the vision, the people needed to remember the call to reach that point in time. They still had to rectify their own problems and align fully with God's appointed areas of life and ministry.

Being part of divine history doesn't require us to be great, or mighty, or perfect. It does require us to be obedient, that big word that often causes us to do a lot of stumbling. Perhaps that is one of the major reasons why God discusses the law in this passage, pointing out their knowledge of the written code that was meant to reveal, rather than conceal, their need for Zerubbabel's ancestor to come and transform their spiritual state.

Israel rebuilt the temple. That temple would, along with much of Israel's remnant return, be destroyed later in time. Israel would fall into sin, much like they had in the past. Rather than looking just at the temple, God wanted Israel to examine themselves and learn a bigger lesson than is found in just the reconstruction of a building. Why Israel hadn't undertaken this project of their own free will and volition in 16 years was just as important as their decision to heed divine instruction and get busy on the building.

God's comparison between desecration and consecration provided the Israelites with yet another mirror of their own conduct and reality. All the things they sought before God in their lives were now idols. They were a defiled people, no longer pure in their relationship with their Creator (Leviticus 18:24, Jeremiah 2:7, Jeremiah 3:9, Jeremiah 32:34). Their behavior, actions, and idolatries led to other spiritual issues, which left everything they offered to God as defiled in His sight. While consecration marks holiness and being set apart for the Lord (specifically for His purpose), desecration marks one who is defiled and a part of the world. The people of Israel were in a state of desecration, whereby everything they touched led to another consequence absent of God's presence.

What are we "touching" that defiles us? People identifying themselves as Christians want a touch of God and then want to go and touch everything that has to do with the world. We want to feel the wind of the Spirit and then rub up with every dollar, car, house, job promotion, date, potential spouse, want, thought, and feel we have. Christians are compromising their very souls and spiritual existences for the sake of money and things! In pursuit of these things, everything such people touch becomes defiled. They cannot offer themselves as temples of the Holy Spirit, because the Holy Spirit does not dwell within them (Jeremiah 4:18, Jeremiah 6:15, Mark 3:29, Acts 7:51, 1 Corinthians 8:7, Ephesians 4:30, Hebrews 12:15). They are not holy but defiled. We can't fool God. Putting on a good church show, church face, and acting all holy in church doesn't mean we act that way outside of church. Our act of praise and worship is defiled if there is nothing behind it, and God will not accept it.

God is calling those who've become distracted by false hopes and desires to return to Him and become a holy, undefiled people. It is within our choice to turn aside from idols and wrongdoing and turn fully to the Lord, making the discipline to follow the leading of the Holy Spirit in our lives. We can't do it without the Spirit, but as the Spirit lives within us, we can live the lives God asks of us. When we miss the mark, we ask for forgiveness and start again, turning our ways to His. We are set apart, holy and chosen, consecrated for Him; now, as with Israel, it is our command to live in such a way that is glorifying to Him (Ephesians 2:2-22).

Understanding the process of defilement is also essential to following the precepts of consecration. Here in Haggai the Lord reveals to us a simple yet often overlooked precept: filth and contamination "rubs off," while holiness does not. The offerings made to God under the Old Covenant law were specifically formulated to stand, meeting specific requirements, and could not be changed, added to, or modified without losing their significance (Deuteronomy

4:2, Deuteronomy 12:32, Leviticus 10:1-20). Holiness is the same way: it requires the sanctification of the individual by the Holy Spirit (2 Thessalonians 2:13), sealed with that seal for the day of redemption (Ephesians 4:30). It involves a person's spirit, mind, will, and emotions in agreement with God. A person cannot be consecrated without their consent. As a result, people do not become holy just because they are around others who are holy. Even though we are called to stand as a witness with our holiness, holiness must be the conscious decision of every individual who seeks God in a profound and sanctifying way. The key is living by God's requirements as we offer ourselves a living sacrifice to God (1 Peter 2:5).

Defilement, however, is a different matter entirely. There is an old expression, "Birds of a feather flock together." This is the principle of defilement. Defilement can happen through our associations, behaviors, or pursuits. Even though we may not plan to defile ourselves, defilement comes through compromises made when believers begin to follow worldly influences and pursue things that lead to life. It occurs whenever a believer starts pursuing something they are not equipped to handle spiritually and begin to think, act, and behave in accord with their worldly influences. An example of defilement would be a man or woman who sees images classified as pornographic and then begin pursuing such scenarios and images in real life. Even though everyone knows pornography is done via acting and various staged effects, one who has been defiled by such truly believes the scenes are obtainable. They think about such things, do such things, and intensely pursue the results. This individual has had the filth of pornography rub off on them, causing themselves to be defiled. What might have seemed innocent, casual, even curious set off an entire chain reaction in this individual, pulling them away from God.

There are an endless number of ways people can experience defilement, which is why God's Word advises us to guard our hearts (Deuteronomy 4:39, Deuteronomy 6:6, Deuteronomy 10:16, Proverbs 4:23). In the case of the Israelites, their defilements came through attachments to things more than God (idolatry). To set themselves aright, they needed to re-consecrate their hearts, minds, actions, and very selves to the ministry of God. Doing such would render God's blessing (Deuteronomy 28:1-14) upon them once again.

The issues of consecration and defilement are the very reason the Scriptures advise us to give careful attention to our thoughts, focus on certain things, and attend to our conducts (Ephesians 4:17, Philippians 4:4-9, 2 Peter 3:1). If we are the temples of the Holy Spirit, our very lives should echo the greatness of God, breathing life on a dying world. The ministry of God should always be our first priority. Through it, we see God's glory and find ourselves centered and focused in His presence.

Haggai 2:15-19

"'Now give careful thought to this from this day on—consider how things were before one stone was laid on another in the LORD's temple. When anyone came to a heap of twenty measures, there were only ten. When anyone went to a wine vat to draw fifty measures, there were only twenty. I struck all the work of your hands with blight, mildew and hail, yet you did not return to Me,' declares the LORD. 'From this day on, from this twenty-fourth day of the ninth month, give careful thought to the day when the foundation of the LORD's temple was laid. Give careful thought: Is there yet any seed left in the barn? Until now, the vine and the fig tree, the pomegranate and the olive tree have not borne fruit.

"'From this day on I will bless you.'"

(Related Bible references: Deuteronomy 28:22, 1 Chronicles 22:19, 1 Kings 8:37, Jeremiah 5:3, Amos 4:6-11, Haggai 1:5, Zechariah 8:9, 1 Corinthians 10:13)

Verses 15-19 call God's people to a place of awareness. Once again, as they were called earlier in Haggai, are they called to give careful thought to their ways. God points out, yet again, they sought certain results, and did not receive them. The blight, mildew, hail, and lack of fruit were a sign of defilement: what they produced, sought, and desired were all defiled. God could not bless them with abundance because they were not seeking first His Kingdom and living consecrated to Him.

These blights were a glaring, flashing sign that the people were not putting God first in their lives. They refused to rebuild the temple and pursued everything but God in the process. Even with all this mounting evidence, the Israelites still refused to return to God. They still pursued their idols and interests for many years.

In every circumstance, God is sending us messages about our situation. The New Covenant tells us God will not allow us to encounter things beyond our ability to handle them (1 Corinthians 10:13). We often speak of this in the context of emotional or spiritual warfare. While it is true in the context of emotional and spiritual warfare, it is also true in a larger sense. If we pursue things that we cannot afford, cannot make fruitful, or cannot produce, they will experience spiritual blight, mildew, hail, and lack of fruit. If we can't afford it, can't make it fruitful, or can't produce it, God hasn't given it to us because it is more than we can handle. Too often believers do not step back in self-assessment, considering if they've missed God in matters or are pursuing things without God's blessing. Just because we want something or have an idea that seems good to us does not mean what we want to pursue is within God's will for us. Having a Kingdom mindset means we approach everything we do in life with the attitude of a greater discovery of God's will. It is essential believers step back when things are not bearing any fruit or seem "blighted" in some way to find God and see whether the things we seek are beyond our abilities.

God resolves to bless the Israelites from that day forward because the Israelites resolved to rebuild and attend to His ministry. They were now ready to be Kingdom builders and ascribed to Kingdom economy. No longer mere visitors to God's Kingdom, they were ready to be blessed as full Kingdom citizens (1 Chronicles 22:19).

Haggai 2:20-23

The word of the LORD came to Haggai a second time on the twenty-fourth day of the month: "Tell Zerubbabel governor of Judah that I am going to shake the heavens and the earth. I will overturn royal thrones and shatter the power of the foreign kingdoms. I will overthrow chariots and their drivers; horses and their riders will fall, each by the sword of his brother.

"'On that day,' declares the LORD Almighty, 'I will take you, My

servant Zerubbabel son of Shealtiel,' declares the LORD, 'and I will make you like My signet ring, for I have chosen you,' declares the LORD Almighty."

(Related Bible references: Song of Solomon 8:6, Isaiah 7:14, Isaiah 42:1, Ezekiel 21:27, Daniel 2:44, Micah 5:10, Malachi 4:1-6, Matthew 1:23, Matthew 1:12-13, Matthew 3:2, Matthew 13:43, Matthew 24:7, Luke 3:27, Luke 9:59-62, Luke 12:49-53, Luke 17:20-21, John 1:1-14, Romans 8:17, Galatians 3:29, Titus 3:7, Hebrews 12:26, 2 Peter 2:1-21, 2 Peter 3:1-18, Revelation 19:1-21)

The prophecy of Haggai ends with a reiteration of the earlier mentioned future prophecy. This time, however, it is specifically addressed to Zerubbabel. It is most appropriate that the prophecy ends with reference and address to this specific figure. As was discussed earlier, Zerubbabel was a special figure, specifically mentioned and spiritually birthed for such a time as his day. Zerubbabel was a prophetic forerunner for Jesus Christ, a part of His ancestry (Matthew 1:12-13, Luke 3:27). Zerubbabel was, therefore, also a part of prophecy in His very life and calling. This prophecy, applying to Christ Himself, speaks again of His power, Kingdom purpose, and His role as the Desire of All Nations.

Believers love to hear about Jesus' return in terms of reward and blessing. It is true the Lord's coming will bring reward and blessing (Malachi 4:1-4, Matthew 13:43, 2 Peter 3:13-18, Revelation 19:1-10). Jesus' coming will also be a time of vindication (Malachi 4:5-6, 2 Peter 2:1-22, 2 Peter 3:1-1-12, Revelation 19:11-21). Just like with the first coming, Jesus' life and presence is both a call to choice and action. As the world shakes, people must choose whether to be defiled by external things or ascribe to God's ways. Every one of us is faced with the choice to follow secular powers, thoughts, fads, religions, teachings, and Kingdoms. We will face decisions about influences, including the influence of close friends and family (Luke 9:59-62, Luke 12:49-53). As the world is shaken, so are our own immediate worlds and circumstances, causing us to question ourselves and assess which Kingdom we, in actuality, follow.

God chose Zerubbabel to serve as an ancestor of the Word made flesh, dwelt among us (John 1:1-14). He is compared to a signet ring, which was a sign of authority. In Biblical times, such was used to confirm the authenticity of divine messages, all of which were stamped by the image found on the ring. It proved ownership of writings, precious articles, and authority. They were always worn on the right hand, and were considered an inseparable possession, one that served as a testament to the owner.

In a bigger sense, signet rings weren't secret. Zerubbabel was not God's covert agent, but one who stood before the world confirmed as a sign in that day and one to come. As God's signet ring, Zerubbabel's very presence proves God transforms lives. This very man who was sown in Babylon was now destined to become the ancestor of Jesus Christ, our Emmanuel (Isaiah 7:14, Matthew 1:23). Where he was sown, where he was born, and where he came from were both relevant and irrelevant at the same time. His place of origin didn't determine his long-term position but also signifies divine transformation at the same time. God had called, and chosen Zerubbabel for a powerful purpose, and a place of power and importance. No matter where he might have come from, Zerubbabel was a leader God could appoint and use.

Zerubbabel's call and appointment in history and Christ's lineage reminds every one of us that being called and chosen is not just about God; it is also about us. Every one of us called and chosen of God must conform ourselves to the life and ministry God has for us. As heirs of Christ, we too are in His lineage and heirs according to His promise (Romans 8:17, Galatians 3:29, Titus 3:7). We can't have a worldly focus, or we will miss God and chase idols. We can't have a self-centered focus, or we will live perpetually chasing want after want, never finding true fulfillment and satisfaction. We can't be overly legalistic, esteeming ourselves by our works and relying on self-righteous rules that divert from God. We can't live disobedient, or we will forever find ourselves alienated from God. We must have a true Kingdom vision, looking forward to the day when our Savior returns.

In the meantime, we wait for Him and attend to the ministry of God, however it manifests for us. If we have turned aside from God's ministry for other things, it is time to hear His call back to rebuild and reestablish His Kingdom within, around, and among us (Luke 17:20-21). We have no more excuses, no more time to waste, no more time to delay His call. The Kingdom of Heaven is at hand, just as much as it was in years past (Matthew 3:2)...are you ready to answer and find your greater purpose in Him?

me labiu electu ut inuocet oms i noie
... burant ei humio uno ... flumina tu ...
el mei fily disptor meor deferent munu ... ...
illa ... cofundis ... cunctis ad muentois; ... ...
... carate ... in me quia ... auferam de medio
magniloquos ... tue ... adiciet exaltari ...
... monte sco meo ... delinque in medio tui po
... paupem ... egenum ... spabunt in noie dni ...
... dr non facient inquitatem nec loquitur
... ... muenietur in ore eor lingua dolo
... pascentur ... accubabunt ... erit qui ...
... dicit dominus lauda filia syon iubila filia
... letare ... exulta ... in omni corde filia ...
... dns iudicium tuum auertit muicos tuos
... dns in medio tui ... timebis malum ultra ...
illa dicet ... noli timere sion non ... dissoluantur
... dns deus tuus in medio tui fortis ... sal
... gaudebit ... te in letitia silebit in dilectoe ...
... exultabit ... te in laude nugas qui a lege recesse
... cogregabo qz ex te erunt ... non bos ultra ... ...
... ecce ego inteficiam oms ... qui
... te in tempore illo ... saluabo claudicam
... ... eam ... erecta ... cogregabo ... ponam eos
... laudem ... nomen ... omni terra cofusiois eor
... illo ... addicam uos ... in tpe quo cogregabo
... dabo uos ... nomen ... in laudem oib;

... restauratioem ... aduen
credulitatem ... uellent ...
... eum ... ... diu ... dum ...
domus dei omnia ... ... tetu hui
... ... poli edificioem tem
... obseruantiam sacerdotalem
... significant ... incipit ...

... anno scdo Dary regis psac
... scm est uerbum domini in ma
... ... filium salathiel ducem
... sacerdotem magnum
... dicens ppl iste dicit ...
... edificandi templum ...
... dicens ... tps uob ...
... ... domus ista deserta ... ...
... corda uestra ... uias uestras
... parum comedistis ...
... estis inebriati opu...
... qui mercedes cogregauit ...
... ... hec dicit dominus exer
... uestras ... ascendite in
... ... edificate domum ... acce
... dixit dominus ...
... est nunc ... itudistis in do
... ... ob cam dic dns exer
... deserta ... uos festinatis in d...

REFERENCES

Introduction References

"Book Of Haggai." http://en.wikipedia.org/wiki/Book_of_Haggai. Accessed on February 13, 2013.

"Haggai." http://en.wikipedia.org/wiki/Haggai. Accessed on February 13, 2013.

Chapter 1

[1] Strong's Exhaustive Concordance of the Bible, #1697
[2] Ibid., #3068
[3] Ibid., #5030
[4] Ibid., #2292
[5] Ibid, #2216
[6] Ibid., #3091
[7] Ibid., #6256
[8] Ibid., #1004
[9] Ibid., #1129
[10] Ibid., #5603
[11] Ibid., #2720
[12] Ibid., #7760
[13] Ibid., #1870
[14] Ibid., #2232
[15] Ibid., #0935

[16] Ibid., #4592
[17] Ibid., #0398
[18] Ibid., #7654
[19] Ibid., #8354
[20] Ibid., #7937
[21] Ibid., #3847
[22] Ibid., #2527
[23] Ibid., #7936
[24] Ibid., #6346
[25] Ibid., #5344
[26] Ibid., #7521
[27] Ibid., #3513
[28] Ibid., #7235
[29] Ibid., #4592
[30] Ibid., #0935
[31] Ibid., #1004
[32] Ibid., #5301
[33] Ibid., #7323
[34] Ibid., #8064
[35] Ibid., #0776
[36] Ibid., #2721
[37] Ibid., #0776
[38] Ibid., 2022
[39] Ibid., #1715
[40] Ibid., #8492
[41] Ibid., #3323
[42] Ibid., #0127
[43] Ibid., #3318
[44] Ibid., #0120
[45] Ibid., #0929
[46] Ibid., #3018
[47] Ibid., #3709
[48] Ibid., #7611
[49] Ibid., #8085
[50] Ibid., #1697
[51] Ibid., #7971
[52] Ibid., #3372
[53] Ibid., #5782
[54] Ibid., #2292
[55] Ibid., #2216
[56] "Zerubbabel." http://en.wikipedia.org/wiki/Zerubbabel. Accessed on February 14, 2013.

[57] Strong's Exhaustive Concordance of the Bible, #3091
[58] Ibid., #7235
[59] Ibid., #0398
[60] Ibid., #7564
[61] Ibid., #7937

Chapter 2

[1] Strong's Exhaustive Concordance of the Bible, #7611
[2] Ibid., #3519
[3] Ibid., #7200
[4] Ibid., #2388
[5] Ibid., #3772
[6] Ibid., #7307
[7] Ibid., #3372
[8] Ibid., #7493
[9] Ibid., #3220
[10] Ibid., #2724
[11] Ibid., #1471
[12] Ibid., 2532
[13] Ibid., #0935
[14] Ibid., #3701
[15] Ibid., #2091
[16] Ibid., #0314
[17] Ibid., #7223
[18] Ibid., #7965
[19] Ibid., #3548
[20] Ibid., #8451
[21] Ibid., #6944
[22] Ibid., #1320
[23] Ibid., #8217
[24] Ibid., #2931
[25] Ibid., #7126
[26] Ibid., #0068
[27] Ibid., #1964
[28] Ibid., #5221
[29] Ibid., #7711
[30] Ibid., #3420
[31] Ibid., #1259
[32] Ibid., #2015
[33] Ibid., #3768
[34] Ibid., #4467

[35] Ibid., #2392
[36] Ibid., #7392
[37] Ibid., #0251
[38] Ibid., #5650
[39] Ibid., #2368
[40] Ibid., #0977

ABOUT THE AUTHOR

DR. LEE ANN B. MARINO, PH.D., D.MIN., D.D.

● ● ● ● ● ● ● ● ● ● ● ● ● ● ● ●

DR. LEE ANN B. MARINO, PH.D., D.MIN., D.D. (she/her) is "everyone's favorite theologian" leading Gen X, Millennials, and Gen Z with expertise in leadership training, queer and feminist theology, general religion, and apostolic theology. She has served in ministry since 1998 and was ordained as a pastor in 2002 and an apostle in 2010. She founded what is now Sanctuary Apostolic Fellowship Empowerment (SAFE) Ministries in 2004. Under her ministry heading Dr. Marino is founder and Overseer of Sanctuary International Fellowship Tabernacle (SIFT) (the original home of National Coming Out Sunday) and The Sanctuary Network, and Chancellor of Apostolic Covenant Theological Seminary (ACTS).

Affectionately nicknamed "the Spitfire," Dr. Marino has spent over two decades as an "apostle, preacher, and teacher" (2 Timothy 1:11), exercising her personal mandate to become "all things to all people" (1 Corinthians 9:22). Her embrace of spiritual issues (both technical and intimate) has found its home among both seekers and believers, those who desire spiritual answers to today's issues.

Dr. Marino has preached throughout the United States, Puerto Rico, and Europe in hundreds of religious services and experiences throughout the years. A history maker in her own right, she has spent over two decades in advocacy, education, and work for and within minority spiritual communities (including African American, Hispanic, and LGBTQ+). She has also served as the first woman on all-male synods, councils, and panels, as well as the first preacher or speaker welcomed of a different race, sexual orientation, or identity among diverse communities. Today, Dr. Marino's work extends to over 150 countries as she hosts the popular *Kingdom Now* podcast, which is in the top 20 percentile of all podcasts worldwide. She is also the author of over 35 books and the popular Patheos column, *Leadership on Fire*. To date, she has had five bestselling titles within their subject matter: *Understanding Demonology, Spiritual Warfare, Healing, and Deliverance: A Manual for the Christian Minister; Ministry School Boot Camp: Training for Helps Ministries, Appointments, and Beyond; Discovering Intimacy: A Journey Through the Song of Solomon; Fruit of the Vine: Study and Commentary on the Fruit of the Spirit;* and *Ministering to LGBTQ+ (and Those Who Love Them): A Primer for Queer Theology* (and its accompanying workbook).

As a public icon and social media influencer, Dr. Marino advocates healthy body image (curvy/full-figured), representation as a demisexual/aromantic, and albinism awareness as a model. Known to those she works with, she is a spiritual mom, teacher, leader, professor, confidant, and friend. She continues to transform, receiving new teaching, revelation, and insight in this thing we call "ministry." Through years of spiritual growth and maturity, Dr. Marino stands as herself, here to present what God has given to her for any who have an ear to hear.

For more information, visit her website at kingdompowernow.org.

www.ingramcontent.com/pod-product-compliance
Lightning Source LLC
Chambersburg PA
CBHW071631040426
42452CB00009B/1578